MW00614570

Endorsements

Dawn Abbott has authored this book to help leaders and entrepreneurs through their business and life challenges by sharing her own experiences. Through thirty-plus years as an entrepreneur, wife, mother, leader, and now an EOS Implementer®, she can make an enormous difference for others like her. Her experiences of struggle, loss, and success give her a unique and impactful perspective.

—Gino Wickman, author of *Traction*® and *The EOS Life*®

Your Life is Not a To-Do List is perfect for these ever-changing times. Dawn flawlessly integrated her heartwarming, personal story into practical Tools that will serve you in your personal and professional growth, no matter your phase in life.

—Rob Dube, founder of a top Forbes Small
Giants company, Author of *Do Nothing*,
Host of *Do Nothing* Podcast

Dawn is one of the most knowledgeable entrepreneurs I have ever encountered, and her book is both inspirational and tactical—exactly what every business owner needs to charge forward. Dawn has a track record of success that gives her the credibility to teach, and yet, as a woman, mother, wife, and daughter, she inspires us deeply with her life experience.

—Brenda Abdilla, PCC Executive Coach/WPO
Chapter Chair

Dawn Abbott's story and guidance have immeasurably touched my life and career. She and I literally walked together through the 2020 recession for miles as she processed that her "entire business model had ceased to exist," and I grappled with the downturn of my own small business. Today, she works with me and my team to march triumphantly forward in our new growth trajectory. Dawn has shown me firsthand what a life well-lived looks like and how a small business made into fun again feels.

—Wendy O'Donovan Phillips, CEO of Big Buzz

As a female entrepreneur, reading this book felt as if I had a personal guide to help me navigate the trials and tribulations along the journey of integrating personal and professional success.

—Erica Spoor, CEO & President, Impact Point Group

The author has written with sheer warmth and candor. Her story will inspire a new entrepreneur or an experienced leader. This book is truly what you need before you make your next important business move.

—Syd Sexton, CEO of Catering by Design

YOUR LIFE IS NOT
A TO-DO LIST

YOUR LIFE IS NOT A TO-DO LIST:

TOOLS FOR A MORE JOYFUL ENTREPRENEURIAL JOURNEY

DAWN ABBOTT

ethos
collective

Printed in the United States of America

Published by Ethos Collective™
PO Box 43, Powell, OH 43065
EthosCollective.vip

LCCN: 2022921247
Paperback ISBN: 978-1-63680-110-0
Hardcover ISBN: 978-1-63680-111-7
e-book ISBN: 978-1-63680-112-4

Available in paperback, hardcover, e-book, and audiobook.

DEDICATION

I dedicate this book to you, the reader. I know you are out there hustling to do excellent work and be great partners, trusted friends, and amazing parents. You are an entrepreneur or leader taking risks, being vulnerable, and putting people first; you inspire me, and I am honored to be a part of this tribe.

CONTENTS

INTRODUCTION

A superb taskmaster, I checked all the boxes and ran life's treadmill faster than most, kicking challenges in the face as soon as they popped up. A to-do list was all I needed. It made sense to be productive, achieve goals, follow the rules, and do everything expected of me. Plus, all that busyness kept me from fully connecting with myself and others because, *yuck*, that is scary and hard. I felt comfortable in the box my productivity created for me. Somewhere along the way, I concluded that to be loved, I must produce. Then life forced me to stop and pay attention.

People who know exactly what they want to do and seem to understand their mission have always impressed me. I merely rolled with it, and it rolled well for a long time. I fell in love with Tim Abbott at age eighteen and married him when I was twenty-one. We had a couple of babies and grew a successful business. The business we began in our two-bedroom townhouse eventually expanded to a fourteen-thousand-square-foot warehouse and a team of employees. Tim and I started two more companies along the way and worked our butts off. We made all the entrepreneurial mistakes, doing it the hard way most of the time. Regardless, we created a good life for ourselves and our kiddos.

In 2012, we had two boys, eighteen and twenty-one years old, and we were thinking about the next chapter in our lives, planning what empty-nesting would look like. Then came the surprise blessing of a new baby. Yep, you heard that right— I was pregnant. Our beautiful daughter was born in May 2013. We had some trepidation about starting over just as we were almost done raising children but were excited about the chance to do it all again.

I thought my toughest challenge that year would be the financial strain of two kids in college and a full-time nanny. However, the universe had other plans for my challenge train. In August 2013, we lost Tim in an accident while on vacation. Here I was, a widow with a three-month-old baby, three businesses, and two young men who had lost their father. That was not the freaking plan for this chapter!

Through a long, rocky road of lessons, I have achieved joy and peace again. I am remarried. My businesses are thriving without me sacrificing my life for them, and I am comfortable being a flawed human with gifts to share. I am a wife, mother, daughter, sister, friend, author, entrepreneur, coach, teacher, and facilitator who makes mistakes and continues to grow every day by the grace of God. Also, I am now a business coach and EOS Implementer* who walks alongside other entrepreneurs as they journey to find clarity, strategy, and healthy mindsets around their lives and businesses. My goal is to share my story and the lessons this path has taught me. My passion is to help each of you live on purpose, become your absolute best, and receive all that you deserve. Each of us can have influence, whether it is changing the world or just helping Mom with the dishes. Please join me in getting to your place of greatest impact.

I have set this book up as part biography and the story of my journey and part learning resource, with some tools at the end of each chapter that have helped me in some of my business and life challenges. It is my hope that you find some of these tools beneficial in your journey; I share my story to encourage you all to share yours. When we share the gift of our experiences, we create a community that helps us see that we are not alone on this roller coaster of life.

I see myself as a sherpa in writing this book. I have been on the trek being a business owner, wife, and mother for well over 30 years and have gained some valuable experience that can help with your trek. However, I am not an expert. I am not a guru. I am still on this journey with you, making mistakes, finding new paths, and learning from each new leg of the trek.

ONE
TIME TO GROW UP

It takes courage to grow up and become who you really are.
—E.E. Cummings

How we grow up affects our entire lives. In the grand scheme of things, our childhood is brief, but I have learned those first eighteen or so years impact everything that follows.

Why do those early years mold everything we do, think, feel, and speak? Our baby brain is like one of those "add water to make it grow" capsules. The experiences of our first eighteen years are the water that melts the coating and unfolds the sponge. The sponge absorbs all the water to maximize its size. As the little sponge physically grows, we learn to do things, such as crawl, walk, run, and eat.

This sponge that is our baby brain also develops a belief system. Everything the sponge experiences contributes to a library of beliefs. With every interaction, our brain takes in the experience and filters it through the belief system we created. This system automatically triggers our reactions and responses based on past experiences. We say, "See, this always happens."

We naturally make assumptions based on what we think we know. But what if we stopped for a moment and considered the facts versus what we accept as truth? Anne Lamott, the author of *Bird by Bird*, refers to the stories we write about our experiences as SFDs, or "Shitty First Drafts."[1] She tells us that everyone creates them, then something happens, and our immediate thoughts, or SFDs, pop up and compel our behavior. These SFDs are what lead to the best drafts that we create later. Think of the possibilities in our interactions if we chose not to see our story through the lens of our old belief library!

GROWING MY BELIEF LIBRARY

My parents were seventeen and eighteen and in high school when I arrived, an obvious accident. They had good intentions and loved me, but they were ill-equipped for adult life, and the first eighteen years of my life were very unstable. I attended eleven different schools because of moves motivated by divorce, new relationships, job losses, or manic whims. My parents were immature and emotionally unhealthy, and they suffered from substance abuse and addictions.

As in-love idealists, my parents thought they had it all figured out, like most teenagers setting off into adulthood. As I understand it, people urged my parents to abort me. And although I did not write this book to take a political stance on the matter or any other political matter, I am most grateful they did not choose that option. They married in October, and I was born in December 1969. I have seen no wedding pictures, but I have beautiful photos of my parents at prom and other school dances.

My mom completed a home correspondence course to finish high school. Dad graduated from high school and went to culinary school. They lived in Huntington Beach, California, and dedicated themselves to my welfare. But wanting a better life for me, they opposed raising me near Los Angeles.

So, after my dad completed chef school, they sold everything and financed a new 1973 Chevy Nova and a pop-up tent trailer. I was three years old when our little threesome set out for the mountains with our cat, Peaches. Over the next six months, we camped, hiked, and drove to see all the western United States sites. I have vague memories from that experience, including some wilderness camping and a few stops at KOA campgrounds to shower, do laundry, and swim in the pool. But most vivid was a feeling of joy and security while climbing rocks on a hiking trail with my parents and our faithful cat. I remember laughing and seeing my parents happy.

As an adult, I admire them for leaving their families and everything they knew at such a young age to create a new life for their daughter. They stopped in Aspen, Colorado, which was a funky little hippy town with great skiing. Aspen was desperate for workers, especially in their burgeoning restaurant industry, so Mom and Dad staked our claim. My dad was a rock star when he pulled into town as a young man who not only had finished culinary school but also was not a ski bum. And employers could tell Dad would do whatever it took to provide for his family. He had several job offers and decided on the executive chef position at the Holiday Inn at the base of the Buttermilk Ski Resort. He eventually became the food and beverage manager for the hotel.

My parents did better than most people expected. They soon bought a four-bedroom house down the road from the mountain homes of Goldie Hawn and Kurt Russell, Jimmy Buffett, Glenn Frey, and other celebrities who had discovered Aspen and all it offered.

I had lots of fun during those years. My memories include helping Dad in the hotel kitchen and falling into a five-gallon bowl of cracked eggs. Mom worked in the restaurant or entertained tourists' kids while their parents skied.

In kindergarten, I would get off the bus at my dad's restaurant, trade my backpack for my skis, and hit the slopes until my parents were ready to go home. Today, I can't imagine letting a five-year-old kid hit the ski slopes alone, but Aspen was a safe little town then, and I always ran into my parents' friends. Many of them were ski instructors who took me for a few runs and taught me how to ski. These were the good years—our little family beat the odds in an amazing environment.

During that time, I made my first entrepreneurial endeavor. Like most entrepreneurs, starting businesses came naturally to me, even when I was very young. I found a field of dying marigolds at the end of summer. So, I picked all the seeds from the dying flowers and put them into baggies to sell to neighbors and teachers. I fondly remember that as the "marigold summer."

My dad worked long hours seven days a week, and he seldom got holidays off. When he didn't have to work, my parents threw parties that involved drugs, drinking, and young people being crazy. The partying became excessive, and the marriage began to fray. My sister, Kimberly, came along when I was six-and-a-half. I believe they hoped she would save their marriage. For my part, I felt I should be extra well-behaved and funny so they would laugh at my cuteness and feel happy. But my efforts did not work; neither baby Kim nor I could save their marriage.

It was around my ninth birthday when my parents sat me down and told me they were splitting up and my dad would be moving out. I felt a sense of relief when my parents recognized they couldn't be together because of their fighting. I hated their fights and felt like a failure when I could not prevent them. But I also felt a rush of fear about the divorce because I knew life would change. Where would I live? Would my sister be with me? Who would get our beloved Golden Retriever, Frito? My parents assured me we would be okay and said they loved me. But it would be many years before I truly felt okay or loved. The next time I felt stable and safe was when I married.

Everything got crazy quickly. My parents sold the house, and my mother left Kim and me with Dad for what seemed like years, even though I know it wasn't that long. To this day, I am not 100% sure where she went. My dad struggled to work and take care of us. He eventually took Kim, Frito, and me to California to be near his sisters so they could help take care of us. We found a little place on the beach, and we had a fun summer.

Near the end of summer, my mom showed up. While happy to see my mom, I was also angry that she had left us. A violent car ride with my parents screaming and hitting each other was how that homecoming ended. The scar of that trauma forever changed me. I wanted to protect my parents from each other, and again, I believed I was not enough to make them okay or for them to love me. That day ended with me leaving with my mom and grandma and being separated from my dad, little sister, and my dog.

That began the ugly court custody battle in Aspen. My parents said terrible things about each other in anger. Eventually, my mom got custody and moved us to Denver with her parents when I was in fourth grade. She worked multiple jobs trying to make ends meet, and we moved three times, which meant attending three elementary schools that year. At one point, we lived in Longmont, Colorado, in an old Victorian house across from my elementary school. My mom would leave for work early, and it was my job to oversee getting my sister out of bed, dressed, and ready for her babysitter to pick her up before I walked to school.

I remember our time in the Victorian house fondly. It was only the three of us girls against the world. Mom was fully present when she wasn't working one of her two jobs. We had a kitten, and my mom had no love interest at the time. When I tell her how much I enjoyed the time in that house, she tells a different story. She talks about how broke we were, how hard she worked, and how scared and lonely she was. I believe how well young children fare during a divorce directly relates to their parents' presence and the quality of time spent with them. I did not know we were struggling financially; I only remember having my mom's attention.

That next summer, my little sister and I visited Dad in Aspen, where he had moved back to a one-bedroom apartment across from the Holiday Inn, where he had gone back to work. He was at the hotel a lot, but we were glad to be there with him and my dog, who was Dad's consolation prize in the divorce. That summer left me with some fond memories. I did not want to leave Aspen or my dad in August to go back to school.

Our Golden Retriever was my dad's best friend during that time, and Frito gave him a reason to live. One night after Kim and I had returned to Denver, our beloved pet ran across the highway, and a car hit and killed him. The loss devastated Dad, and he began his deep dive into addiction. At his worst, he was dealing cocaine to locals, politicians, the sheriff, tourists, Hollywood stars, bigwigs, and everyone else in Aspen, while smoking an excessive amount daily himself.

The following summer, when we visited Aspen, my dad had a bigger apartment and a live-in girlfriend named Gail, a chain smoker who never wanted children. To say the relationship between his girlfriend and his daughters was weird is an understatement. The dynamic had changed for sure. We went to camps and had fun running around town. My sister attended Wildwood, an exceptional preschool in Aspen.

Thank goodness I was helping at the preschool on the day my strung-out father sent a brown paper bag full of marijuana with my sister rather than the bag that had her lunch in it. She opened it and showed me. I shared my lunch with her and kept the bag a secret from the teachers.

Even at that age, I knew what could have happened had I not been there to intercept the weed bag. I brought it home and let my dad watch me dump it into the toilet while I yelled at him about how the authorities could take us away and arrest him for such mistakes.

While we were in Aspen with Dad, my mom moved to Conifer, a small mountain town about an hour from Denver. She moved in with a boyfriend—a loud, giant man who smoked pot in the house and offered me a toke more than once. What a loser!

I enjoyed living in the mountains and my new school. But after our next summer's visit to Aspen, we returned to a new house and a new boyfriend. This one would later become my stepdad and the father of my half-sister.

In my sixth-grade year, my dad came out to visit and told me he was moving back to California. He promised to contact me as soon as he could. I did not end up hearing from him for about two-and-a-half years after that last visit. During his silence, Dad married Gail, and they got themselves clean of substances.

Those years between sixth and ninth grade were stable. My mom had married Mike, who was financially successful. I changed schools only three times, and there were no evictions, roommates, or utility shut-off notices.

I missed my dad and was angry with him, but like most middle school kids, I was self-absorbed and insecure. I loved ninth grade; it was the top grade of West Jeff Junior High. I had lots of friends and a boyfriend and was voted class clown along with a classmate named Trey Parker—yes, *the* Trey Parker of *South Park* fame. Apparently, he went on to do something major with his comedy; I just crack jokes every so often.

My teenage years were often tumultuous. I associated fitting in with being loved, and I enjoyed boys' attention, which later left me feeling empty and even less worthy. Like many girls, I developed body-image issues in middle school. My teen years brought a voice inside my head telling me I was not pretty enough, smart enough, good enough—just not enough. Those years can be so painful. I put on an air of being a fun, crazy girl. I dealt with my introversion and self-consciousness by pretending to be overly extroverted and wearing the class-clown mask.

Once while in middle school, I made a skirt in Home Economics from a GUESS™ pattern. I was immensely proud of the outcome and wore it often. One day, I was waiting for a bus in my homemade skirt. When the bus arrived, I stood up and picked up my bag. I took one step towards the bus full of other teens on their way to school and tripped, falling face down in the gravel. I tried to get up when I realized I had tripped on my skirt, which had fallen to my ankles. So, not only was I on the ground, but I was also in my underwear. I will never forget that moment. My heart raced, tears fell uncontrollably, and the heat of horrific embarrassment pulsed through my body. I got up, pulled my skirt up, and ran home. I did not tell my mom. Instead, I left the house and hid every day until she left for work. I did not go back to school until the school called. My mom was livid and forced me to go back to school.

Now I can look back on that day and laugh. I share that story because it is hilarious for one. I put it in this book because, after all these years, my perspective has changed. That incident became a moment that shaped me. Remembering the pain has helped me determine to never again be that poor girl who wanted to stop living because people saw her in an embarrassing situation. Instead, I want to create a world where everyone recognizes they have done dumb things and made mistakes. If we can learn to be open about them, we will see we're all only human, and we'll be able to love one another as we allow each person to be themselves.

Eventually, my mom divorced Mike, and while she was single, she set very few rules and gave me a loose curfew. I thought her absence was great, but it meant I had too much autonomy for a teen and ample time to make my own choices, not always good choices. I indulged in typical teenage foolishness, trying to fit in and find my tribe.

During my sophomore year, I transferred from a tiny mountain school where I knew everyone to the biggest high school in Denver. With a student body of four thousand, my true introvert came to life in full force. I was afraid to speak to anyone. No one noticed me or knew I was a new kid; we all saw twenty unfamiliar faces a day in those hallways. Thankfully, I pleaded with my mom to let me go to St. Mary's Academy, an all-girls Catholic school, for my junior and senior years, where we had a class of one hundred girls. That school made a significant impact on who I became. The absence of male bravado and female competition was empowering for me. Statistically, girls get less attention than boys from teachers. But at St. Mary's, we got all the teachers' time, attention, and mentorship. I thought being educated with all girls was outstanding. I also worked twenty to thirty hours a week while in high school because I enjoyed having money and freedom (again, some entrepreneurial traits). At St. Mary's, I still portrayed myself as a crazy girl, and as a result, I did not apply myself to my schoolwork or anything extra-curricular besides work and parties.

I wanted to be a teacher or a psychologist; however, SATs, college applications, and paying tuition were not really what I wanted to focus on at that point, and no one held me accountable for doing anything about it. I was not sure what I would do after graduation, but I believed someday I would get a degree and get serious about life. My pattern of work, parties, and helping with my little sisters continued while I lived in my mom's basement with little direction. That is where I was when my next phase of life began.

If you look at your youth with regret and want to forget some choices, remember that each one played a part in helping you become who you are. Every day and experience adds one more puzzle piece that completes us. If you are not proud of some parts of your life, I want you to know you are not alone. Do you still carry that heavy burden? It might be time to let it go. Pick up a piece of paper and let anything from your past that is not serving you flow from the pen. When you've recorded it all, crumple the paper and make a deep, conscious choice to let it go, then drop it. Sometimes all it takes to let go of something is to decide to let it go. The process of forgiving yourself and others from your past can bring up some painful memories, but the freedom this creates is worth the effort.

REWRITING MY BELIEF LIBRARY

When I look back, I can see that what I thought was outgoing, bold, and super fun behavior was actually me hiding my vulnerability and self-consciousness behind the make-'em-laugh coping strategy. I ran through the halls, yelling, making a scene, and causing a commotion wherever I went. Rather than truly connecting and getting close to my peers, I would crack jokes. I was the life of the party. As an adult introvert, at one point, after experiencing the pain and suffering of a networking event, I thought, *what happened to that crazy ninth grader who would do anything for a laugh?* First, I think everyone loses some of their bold, fun selves as they grow up to avoid embarrassment and judgment. Second, I was always an introvert, but to fit in, get attention, and avoid sharing the real mess of my life, I put on the fun "crazy girl" mask. There has been this balance for me in discovering my true self. On the one hand, I want to encourage the child in me to come out and have some more fun, be freer, and more fearless; while on the other hand, I want to ensure that I do not fall into unhealthy coping behaviors like hiding my true self behind a persona that is not really me. My goal is to remember who I was at 6-8 years old when I was most free and try to give that little girl her chance to shine, allowing grownup-me to be my true self and appreciate the strengths of my introversion

I also became a comedian at home. I loved watching my mom laugh at my impersonations and seeing her pride when she would ask me to put on a show and entertain her friends. I also hated every minute of being in the spotlight, but it was worth it to get her affection and approval. That crazy-girl comedian still shows up when I am particularly nervous about a group function. I must remind my inner tween and my grown-up self that while being the class clown protected me when I was fifteen, the only way to true connection and belonging is to just be me. Putting on a show will not make me more loved. I don't want to work to fit in and get attention anymore; I want to be me and find those people who like me for me. I still find joy, however, in helping people laugh, and I have been told by those who get to know me well I am quite comedic.

I spent a lot of time wishing my life had been different, or I had been given a different family. This drafted a lot of my belief library, including books entitled *Not Good Enough* and *I Have No Value*. I believed that productivity and doing everything for everyone brings love. My belief library also assigned me the job of peacemaker and keeping everyone happy and safe. My childhood created some powerful limiting beliefs.

But it also formed some empowering beliefs. My parents gave me my strong work ethic. Both were incredibly hardworking and self-sacrificing. On the one hand, I am grateful for that sense of pride in my work and the understanding that I must put in the effort. They showed me that a strong work ethic is valuable and necessary in starting and running your own business.

However, I have come to see how their efforts helped me write another false narrative in my belief library as well. Unfortunately, my parents lacked the typical success that should have been the product of hard work. This created a belief that working harder is valued over working smarter, and regardless of how hard you work, you never win. I have had to do some work to shed those beliefs. As a new business owner, I worked longer and harder than necessary, often not stopping to think about how I could be smarter in my efforts versus just working more.

I have spent my life being fiercely independent, with an intense need to be productive, helpful, and resilient. I want to take care of people even when they may not want or need me to. However, I struggle with accepting help from others. Those traits have been incredibly helpful while running a family and multiple businesses.

Nevertheless, this trait of wanting to take care of others has a flip side. I have an unhealthy need to maintain control, and my self-value is erroneously linked to checking boxes and accomplishing tasks. My needs and emotions get pushed to the back burner in my relationships because the needs of others must come first.

I have come to understand that my need to help people and give to those around me can show up as a form of manipulation. While I appreciate that one of my core values is to help others, not all my giving is altruistic. My belief library tells me giving and doing things for others brings love, attention, appreciation, and accolades. As I grow, I remind myself to check my motives before I say yes to something self-sacrificing. I remind myself that every yes will force me to say no to something else, so I must keep my time choices sacred. I try to make choices not to do for others just to be liked or to get appreciation. I work to only put their needs first if doing so truly aligns with my values and can be a win/win for all.

Our belief library is strong; even when we know it is in our best interest, it can be scary to let go of the familiar identity we have created. But growing up means giving up that which is comfortable and has served us well so we can go after everything we truly want in this life.

As I look back at my childhood now, I can let go of what I wished my family had been. I have forgiven my parents because I genuinely believe they did the best they could. I did not always feel that way. There were times when I thought, *why could my parents not have done better? Why didn't they get their act together?* Now I try to remind myself that they did their best with who they were and the tools they had. They did their best with their capacity.

Admittedly, I fight with that truth quite often. Something my parents might say triggers me, and I want to lash out with anger, blame, and hurt. There have been moments when I did just that. I felt regret afterward because that is not who I want to be. Letting my "Shitty First Drafts" control my behavior does not help me, my parents, our relationship, or even my relationships with my husband and children. I love my parents, and I appreciate who they are because they helped form who I am now. I can honestly look back and say if they had been the perfect parents that I dreamed of, I might be a train wreck because my rebellious nature would have overtaken the responsible rule follower in me. Don't get me wrong; I was far from perfect, but I knew I did not want to follow their example, so I made mostly good decisions.

We must peel back the onion to understand where our behaviors originate. Whether those behaviors are ones that we appreciate or ones that we want to change, we must first understand where they came from. What we must not do is become a victim of them. We can't use our past as an excuse not to be who we were created to be. I could choose to have a crutch that includes a childhood plagued by instability, then perpetuate that lifestyle. But ultimately, that would be on me because *grownups get to choose their lives.*

Rewriting your belief library takes work. I am far from done with this work. Just when I am sure I have gotten rid of something from my past that is not serving me, a new deeper scar shows up for me to work on. My intentional effort is what took me from being angry at my parents and their choices to accepting that they are humans with flaws, just like me. Making intentional choices, some therapy, and lots of prayers have allowed me to say, "I no longer want my past experiences to control my thoughts and behaviors." Growing past my belief library helps me understand that struggles are gifts from God, as much as blessings are. Because of this work, the lessons learned have brought contentment and forced me to reframe my limiting beliefs and take responsibility for my choices. I have been given the gift of creating the life I want, not just living with whatever circumstance I am given. I get to choose to have control of my life.

It can be scary to give up being the victim and surrender the identity of the person with a troubled past. I used to cling to these identities because they gave me a story, allowing my ego to feel resilient as I shared how I rose above. Becoming someone vulnerable who wanted a real connection with others meant giving up that character I created to feed my ego.

Being vulnerable allowed me to be who I really am. I write in the past tense, but all this work is ongoing. It is part of my present and my future. I don't think there is a door I will walk through one day that will allow me to stop working on myself; I will always be a work in progress.

TOOLS FOR A JOY-FILLED LIFE

Tool #1

Revise Your Belief Library

Dealing with your limiting-belief library, understanding the stories you have created, and taking responsibility for yourself and how you have labeled yourself is a critical first step.

We must watch what we say about ourselves. Remember, if you tell a girl she is stupid enough times, she will believe it even if she just taught herself to speak Chinese.

Step One: Love yourself and take credit for all of you—the good, bad, and ugly. Try to be grateful for your past rather than angry about it. Think about what it taught you.

Pat yourself on the back for all your accomplishments, and take responsibility for every mess you have created along the way as well. Remember all that you learned from all of it.

Step Two: Start noticing the messages you tell yourself, the excuses that pop up when you dream about what you want. Pay attention to those times when you say, "I can't because . . ." or, "I would love to _____, but . . ."

"I can't start a business because . . ."

"I am alone because . . ."

"I don't have enough money because . . ."

"I'd love to work on what I'm passionate about, but I need to make money."

"I want a better relationship with my spouse, but he/she never listens to me."

Step Three: Every self-limiting belief has a flip side. All the experiences in your life combined to create your disempowering beliefs, but they have created empowering beliefs, also. Spend some time thinking about what these are for you.

Here is my personal example:

Limiting belief: *I must produce and do things for others to be loved.*

Empowerment from the same experiences: *I am productive, I like to help people, and it feels good. I am also worthy of love, even if I do not want to work today, and even if I need to say no to helping right now.*

Both statements can be true, but one holds me back, while one lifts me.

Here is another example of reframing your belief:

Limiting belief: *I'd love to work on what I'm passionate about, but I need to make money.*

Empowering belief: *I'd love to work on what I'm passionate about, and I'll find a way to make money doing it.*

Even your empowering belief may not be perfect, but I promise that empowering-belief systems will take you further than limiting ones.

ANOTHER WAY TO WORK ON THAT BELIEF LIBRARY

Between stimulus and response, there is a space. In that space is our power to choose our response. In our response lies our growth and our freedom.
—Viktor E. Frankl

Our goal is to find another way to look at our limiting beliefs. I learned the following method from studying the work of Brené Brown and taking a certification class for delivering workshops on *Everything DiSC® Productive Conflict* and *Everything DiSC® Agile EQ*.

Think about the last time you had an interaction with someone, and it did not turn out as you hoped. What happens when you feel yourself getting emotionally hooked? You feel strong emotions, your heart races, and you get hot and flushed. Do you remember having immediate assumptions or strong emotions about what that interaction meant?

Let's say you are excited about a new idea, and you share it in a meeting with your work team. They say, "Okay, let's talk about this later." Now you are emotionally hooked. Your mind tries to process what they meant. You tell yourself: *Oh my gosh, what did I say? I must have totally screwed up. They hate my ideas; they think I am stupid.* Or you create some other horrible version of the truth. We do this because our limiting beliefs are strong, and we need to prove they are true. We jump to conclusions, and this causes trouble. Our emotions lead to our thoughts, and those thoughts then dictate our actions and behavior. We must look at all three—emotions, thoughts, and actions—and then make intentional tweaks to each to be our best selves.

The next time you feel triggered by strong emotions about something and have created a scenario in your head about what you think is true, follow these steps.

OVERCOMING THE LIMITING-BELIEFS PROCESS

1. **Feel it.** First, write the scenario you created. What does this feel like for you? Why are you emotionally hooked? Why are you thinking about this rather than going about your day? Using the example about your work team's response to your idea. Write down how you feel and the story that you made up in your head.

2. **Understand it.** Define your feelings. Don't limit yourself to terms such as happy, sad, angry, excited, or scared. Go outside the box, dig deep, and define what you are feeling (e.g., fear of rejection, inadequacy, resentment, worry about whether you are doing the right things in your role/life).

3. **Know its source.** This is about understanding the experiences from your past that may skew your perception of what is happening now. Consider the meeting example again, where a perceived brush-off was so upsetting. If you grew up surrounded by people who literally jumped for joy to express their enthusiasm, then you may be disappointed by any reaction that is more restrained. Likewise, if you were once unexpectedly let go from a job after presenting ideas you thought were well-received, then you may likely be paranoid when given a neutral response to your ideas. We must learn to recognize when past experiences might be shaping our reactions in the present and why.

4. **Learn from it.** We create these stories to prove we are right about our beliefs. We developed those beliefs based on past experiences. Take a minute to learn from what your emotions and thoughts are teaching you about yourself and your beliefs. These moments are a perfect place to start learning more about yourself.

5. **Reframe it.** What if these experiences didn't cloud your point of view? Let's revisit that team reaction experience and only include what is 100% fact. The truth is, we have no idea what your teammates were thinking. Their response may have had nothing to do with the idea you presented. Now, what choices can you make based on this new truth? You could call the team and ask how they felt. You could ask if you did anything wrong or if you should be concerned. This new perspective offers a variety of choices because you took the time to understand the difference between the story your limiting beliefs created and the true facts of the experience.

We start by feeling and understanding our emotions, but we can't stop there. We must also be intentional about changing the thoughts created by the emotion. Lastly, we change how we choose to behave. As a bonus, we learn something about the limiting beliefs we carry, and we can start to eliminate the blocks they are creating in our life.

Tool #2

Change the Locus of Control

I learned about the locus of control when I was in a business incubator program through the Small Business Development Center. Jim Dethmer, Diana Chapman, and Kaley Warner-Klemp, the authors of *The 15 Commitments of Conscious Leadership*, call the concept of above-the-line and below-the-line-leadership "the most important model we know of for being a conscious leader."[2]

We have the power to shift the locus of control above the line. Above-the-line thinking uses the acronym O.A.R. When we take Ownership, Accountability, and Responsibility for ourselves, our choices, and our lives, we set ourselves up for more joy.

Below-the-line thinking uses the acronym B.E.D. If we continue to Blame others, make Excuses, and Deny there is a problem, our lives will be full of what others dump on us. When we live with a victim's identity, we deny ourselves the opportunity to take responsibility for our own lives. If you look at the whole of your life from the perspective of what your part was, you will have the ability to change and mold the future.

I once drove an hour for a scheduled appointment with a client. When they were not there, I was annoyed. I reviewed the emails and found I was at the right place and time. I could have said, "See, it's not my fault; this stuff always happens to me; it's Murphy's law, yadda, yadda." Instead, I changed my locus of control. From that moment on, I took ownership and responsibility for my part in the appointment process. I am accountable for confirming appointments before I drive anywhere. Now that type of frustrating situation rarely happens.

While that is a small example, think of the difference your perspective of control can make on the important things in your life. I could blame my parents for failed marriages using the excuse that it's not my fault because I've never been shown a healthy relationship. Instead, I changed my locus of control, found people in the kind of loving marriage that I wanted, and learned from them. I take responsibility, fight harder for my marriage, and do not allow myself to give up.

Where can you see yourself in a BED of blame, excuses, and denial? Are you blaming others for your choices, making excuses for why you are not doing what it takes, or denying you have a part in your own problems? It is time to grab an OAR and take ownership for yourself, your decisions, the life you want to live, and how you behave. Remember, you are a grown-up, and how your life looks is up to you. *You* get to choose. I invite you to stop and consider your reactions when negative events occur in your life. What is your reaction? Do you launch into blaming someone or something else? Do you try to defend yourself or come up with the "reason" (or excuse) that it happened? Do you find yourself denying that you may be part of the problems that you experience? Again, as the Viktor Frankl quote states, what might be different if you stop and start with the question, "What was my part in this?" When I have done this, I have an opportunity to make some tweaks in the way I am living to improve my interactions and my life experiences in a positive way.

TWO
LIFE'S EXPECTATIONS

Intentional living is the art of making our own choices before others' choices make us.

—Richie Norton

I met the man of my teenage dreams, Tim Abbott, while working at a catering company. He was twenty-four with a place of his own and my super-cute boss. The only problem was that at work, he was focused on getting the job done and getting out of there. He never showed any sign of attraction or that he even thought about me. In fact, he was not necessarily very nice to me; you might say he was standoffish.

Tim oversaw all catering operations—making sure deliveries were done and the equipment and food got to all events. Unsure of my title, I was told to just help him. About two weeks after I started, we had a week from hell. The catering company we worked for was doing all the concessions and private events for the Castle Pines International Golf Tournament, plus that year's Parade of Homes concessions and various regular parties and events. We put in about 120+

hours of extremely arduous labor that week. We worked from four each morning until after midnight. For two nights that week, we slept in the warehouse. I was being paid hourly, so on payday, I was ecstatic. Tim, on the other hand, was on salary. He said, "I made twenty-five cents per hour, F this!" And no one saw him for the next three days.

When our manager told me to go to Tim's house and find out if he was coming back to work, I started by asking around about him. I was not going to just knock on this man's door and ask him about the status of his employment. At eighteen, right out of high school, it would be embarrassing. Well, everything was embarrassing at that age and level of insecurity, but seriously, knock on his door?

I learned that he had just been evicted because the roommate in charge of paying rent had been collecting but not paying. He had just worked like a slave and needed to find a place to live! On top of all that, it was his birthday.

So, my plan was to wish him a happy birthday and see if there was anything I could do to help. I took balloons and a card to his home, but he wasn't there, so I left them on the porch.

He appreciated the gesture so much that he called to thank me and ended up asking me out. We went to a dive bar where he knew I wouldn't get carded. By the time we finished our first date, I was concerned about him driving me home. So, I offered to drive, and that was the beginning of our romance.

Tim never really tried to win me over. Oblivious to my attraction and aloof to women, he worked, partied, and chased adrenaline in his free time. He didn't need a girlfriend. His lackadaisical attitude made me never want to let him go, and the challenge of making him like me was intoxicating.

Colorado is an amazing place for an adrenaline junkie like Tim. On our second date, he took me cliff-jumping at a reservoir in the mountains. We had to climb a forty-foot cliff protruding over a freezing mountain lake, then jump off a precarious ledge into the icy water. The fact that I had done this plenty of times in Aspen with my parents when I was young made me look cool in my new boyfriend's eyes, even though it was not my favorite form of entertainment.

Tim was exhilarating—he made me work for his attention, lived his true self without apology, and offered a bit of danger. All his adrenaline-seeking, rule-breaking, and indifference made him more desirable. My personality of stability, responsibility, and the need to take care of people balanced him nicely.

We moved in together just three months after jointly jumping off cliffs for the first time. Two years later, he put an engagement ring on my finger after asking me to marry him at a different dive bar (how romantic). I found myself skeptical we would ever really marry. I loved him, and I knew he loved me, but he had issues with partying and alcohol with which I couldn't compete. If I had been a little more mature, had more self-esteem, or had a different upbringing, I might have left him. I look back now and think, "Thank God I was young and dumb, so I stuck around." You see, Tim gave me an amazing twenty-five years, three beautiful children, a career, a partnership, and a roller coaster ride of ups and downs that I am blessed to have had.

Though flawed like the rest of us, Tim was a wonderful man, full of integrity, strength, resilience, and a great heart. His cyclical alcohol problem proved to be a thorn in our sides throughout our life together. A very functional alcoholic, he remained successful in his career, as a husband and father, and socially. Alcoholism never caused enough pain for him to give up drinking entirely. He often realized it impeded him, keeping him from being all that he wanted to be, so he would quit for a while. But after a time, it would pop up with its ugly hold on him.

I vowed that I would hang from a bridge by my toes before I would ever separate my family or create instability for them. I swore I would never allow my kids to experience what I went through when my parents divorced, but I think my focus on being the perfect family was as much for me and my need for stability as it was for my family.

Before Tim and I got married or even set a date, I found out I could not have children. Doctors informed me that medical intervention would be needed when I was ready to get pregnant, with little guarantee that it would ever happen. But just after my twenty-first birthday, I started gaining weight, throwing up all the time, and feeling exhausted. I finally went to the doctor, assuming I had something dramatic, like a gastrointestinal disease. Instead, I found out I was four months pregnant. The news caused trepidation and excitement. I had dreamed of being a mom and thought my earlier diagnosis had stolen that from me.

This God "wink" of the gift of a son told me God knew that Tim and I should stay together. When Tim arrived home to our basement-level studio apartment, I sat him down and said, "Here is the deal. Either you are all in or I will set you free and expect nothing from you in the future." I did not want my child to have a half-time dad or shared custody. I was determined to create a different life for this miracle baby than I had growing up. We would be a real family, or I would go it alone. He said, "All in," without hesitation. From that moment on, Tim was always 100% in as a dad and husband. We got married in my grandma's backyard four months before Joshua was born.

The birth of our first child was a huge lesson in letting go and loving what comes. We had attended Lamaze classes and written our birth plan, and it was going to be a moment that we would remember as a perfect, beautiful experience forever. Well, when I went into labor, we went to the hospital, hung out for four hours with no change, and the doctors sent us home saying, "Come back when it hurts so bad that you can't walk." Now I will be darned if I will be a wimp. Twenty-four hours later, the time came when it hurt so bad that I could not walk. Tim was installing a toilet in our new home.

"It's coming NOW!" I yelled.

"Don't worry, I will carry you to the car," Tim said.

"It will either be here or in the Honda," I replied.

After peeking, he said, "The head is almost out," and he called 911. Our son was born in our home twenty minutes before the paramedics came to take us to the hospital. So much for that beautiful birth plan. Instead, we ended up with a unique birth story that I love sharing. It was quite beautiful—just not in the way that I expected. It is also cool for my son that his dad's name is on his birth certificate as "attending."

During those first years of marriage, I feel like I let expectations dampen the light of life. When Tim and I started our life together, we were lucky to scrape together enough spare change for the extras. We put everything we could into buying our first home, which we moved into seven days before our first son was born. We did not spend anything on luxuries.

At one point, when the business had started to show real promise, and we had a little extra in the bank, we decided to go to a special event conference in Las Vegas. We had never taken a vacation, and I had never been to Las Vegas. I lost weight, bought a new dress, got a fake tan, and had my nails done. By the time we boarded the plane, my expectations for this trip were higher than the sky.

Las Vegas let me down. It was not the glamorous place I had imagined. The fancy evening out turned out to be a poorly executed conference dinner. I ended up sitting on the floor in my fancy new dress, eating sub-par convention-center food from a buffet. My wonderful, fiscally responsible husband did not want to pay for a cab back to the hotel. He said, "You can see it right down the street." Unfortunately, the hotel that looked like it was a block away was about three miles; the Vegas Strip is tricky like that. My fancy new shoes became torture devices.

The vacation never got better. Even if it had not been terrible, that vacation could never have met my expectations. I would have been disappointed, regardless.

For many years I continued living a life full of expectations for myself and those around me. I made plans as if I could control all the outcomes in my life. That thinking leads to disappointment and undue stress.

I see so many people (especially women) who have a huge, unrealistic expectation of themselves, their lives, and the people in their lives. We truly have this idea that we can have it all and be it all. We feel guilty when we are with our families and not at work, and we feel guilty when we are working and not with our families.

If we are to find joy, we must give ourselves grace and manage our expectations for ourselves and the expectations of our big messy lives. Joy comes when we realize it may not turn out as we expect but that there will be beauty to be found in whatever may happen if we look for it.

"Unrealistic expectations are potentially damaging because they set us and others up for failure," says Selena C. Snow, Ph.D., a clinical psychologist in Rockville, Maryland. When we or someone else naturally falls short, we draw false conclusions, feel difficult feelings, and act in unhelpful ways", she adds.[3]

I've learned to embark on every trip, big moment, adventure, new project, and relationship with this thought: *I am open and curious to learn, I will be present, I will enjoy the time, and I understand it is just one moment in a lifetime of other moments.* This shift in thinking allows most things I do to exceed my expectations.

TOOLS FOR A JOY-FILLED LIFE

Tool #3

Manage Your Expectations

Step One. Write two lists of all the expectations you currently have. One should contain everything expected of you—by yourself and by all those in your life. The next list will include the expectations you have for the people around you. When I made my first list, it covered three notebook pages— over one hundred expectations. No wonder I was stressed! I wrote down things such as always having a clean house and full fridge; cooking healthy, well-balanced meals every day; never letting my stress bother anyone else; making sure my team always loved their job; never giving up; and on and on and on. As for my second list, I realized that my expectations for others would require them to read my mind, know my preferences, and do everything exactly the way I thought it should be done. *How unrealistic was all of that? Jeez!*

Step Two. Examine each expectation. Can each one logically be expected of you or others?

Step Three. Work through the list and determine how each expectation was created. Did you make it up? Was it created falsely by your beliefs, society, etc?

Step Four. Take each false or unrealistic expectation and get rid of all these items that are illogical and robbing you of joy.

Step Five. The expectations that remain should be true and real. Ask yourself these questions:

1. Can I live up to this?

2. Do I want to live up to this?

3. Will it matter in a year, a week, or even tomorrow if I or someone else lives up to this expectation?

4. What action steps will I take to revise it, get help with it, or let it go?

Step Six. Create a new list of ten or fewer expectations for yourself and no more than ten for the other people in your life. Make sure each one is truly one of the most important to you. Each expectation should honor your values, allow you to use your gifts, and help you move your vision forward. My expectations for myself have been reduced to:

1. Have faith—a belief that everything is as it is supposed to be.

2. Be present.

3. Learn and grow.

4. Love well and be loved.

5. Do unto others as *they* want done unto them.

6. Practice empathy.

7. Help altruistically.

8. Be humble and confident.

9. Be me/Be real.

10. Have more faith—not only that everything is as it should be, but also that God has it all figured out.

That is all. I must remind myself often of the top ten when I feel expectations creeping into my conscious thought. If anybody needs or expects anything more than this list from me, they may or may not get it.

I also do not expect others to be anything more or less than who they are being. This keeps me from disappointment. When someone lets me down, I simply determine if this is who they always were. If the answer is yes, then it's high time to quit expecting something different. I have learned that when actions and words are incongruent, believe the actions. Secondly, I must always remind myself to provide clarity of my expectations to others. I then must provide them with the space to decline or ask me to revise my expectations of them. I have found that it is unfair of us to expect people to say yes unless they feel they are free to say no. I think we are all familiar with those times when we get the message that the request we have received is not actually a question but an order that we do something. What happens is disappointment on both sides because we are not committed to our "required" yeses. I now realize that if I am requesting something from someone, I must be ready to be denied and make sure I can handle that. I also cannot expect something from someone when I have not clearly stated my expectation of them. For example, we want our significant other to hear clues and somehow read our minds to get us the exact birthday present we want, leaving us disappointed when we do not get it. How about we just ask for what we want and set them up for success? Or keep being disappointed. You choose.

THREE
TAKING THE LEAP

Courage is fear that has said its prayers.
—Dorothy Bernard

Tim and I started our business, Fun Productions, in 1991. We were young, had no college degrees, were barely making ends meet, and had just become new parents. It started as a side hustle so I could stay at home with our baby boy.

Tim worked his full-time job and did Fun Productions' events after work. With $3000 my dad gave us, Tim built four casino tables. Then we trained some friends to deal blackjack, craps, and roulette tables, and off we went to become a casino event company. I made calls to venues and caterers while our new baby napped, and we covered events on nights and weekends. It wasn't easy, but we were young, had a great work ethic, and were determined to be the family neither of us had growing up.

We were scared and doubted ourselves every day. But our little fledgling business grew. At one event, the event planner brought in a Velcro Wall, a Bungee Run, and Human

Bowling from Los Angeles. Tim had a lightbulb moment. He believed we could be the first in Denver to offer this type of thing for special events. I knew he was running with this idea with or without my help. So, I got on board and wrote a great business plan with a template software I bought, and we went to thirteen banks.

Not surprisingly, we were heartbroken when financial institutions refused to take a risk on two uneducated kids with no business experience who wanted to buy a Velcro Wall. I moved on and figured the dream was over. I started a preschool in our house to help with the bills and planned to save and grow slowly with our side business. But Tim did not give up that easily.

My husband borrowed $5000 from his mom and made it our emergency fund. Then he filled out multiple credit card applications. He was making a business mistake of taking out short-term debt to provide long-term capital for a business start-up. However, he knew what most people did not. He was betting on us and going all in because he knew we were worth the risk.

One day he walked up to the house with an air hockey table on a dolly. Surprised, I said something like, "Why aren't you at work, and why do you have an air hockey table that will not fit in here?" He explained that he had quit his job and was going full steam ahead to expand the business. I found out he had purchased other equipment without me knowing. I don't think I was ever as enthusiastic or excited about events as he was, but I had to roll with it or get rolled over by it. So, I again jumped on his dream and started the process of booking events for the garage full of equipment that continued to arrive.

Through the help of fertility treatments, we were blessed with another baby boy in 1995. The business had grown, and we were remarkably busy trying to manage it all. The night we brought Hogan home from the hospital, Tim dropped us off and immediately left for an event. I took one week of maternity leave and was back to work with a newborn in tow. That was the season we were in, the start-up phase where we thought everything else came second to building the business.

The grind of building Fun Productions was beyond what most people would likely be willing to do. With no experience or education in business, we worked unbelievably hard. Our one-hundred-hour work weeks often included shifts of thirty-five-plus hours. The business required physical stress as we loaded and unloaded trucks, set up equipment, and worked the events, as well as constant mental challenges in the planning, marketing, and administration of a small business.

ENTREPRENEURIAL SELF-DOUBTS

As we began our endeavor, I dealt with terrible self-talk: "Who are you to think you can have a business?" "Make sure no one knows how inadequate you are; they will never sign a contract." We sometimes look around and think we do not deserve this life we have or are not capable of creating the life we want. The "imposter syndrome" kicks in, telling us we are not enough for this life. If you are anything like me, you have had those moments of questioning, *am I good enough for this?* Or thinking, *I am a fraud, and everyone is going to find out.* You are not alone; up to 82% of high-achieving people are said to have faced some level of feeling like they are not good enough, even though their achievements prove otherwise. Imposter syndrome, also called perceived fraudulence, involves feelings of self-doubt and personal incompetence that persist despite your education, experience, and accomplishments.[4]

When we face that kind of internal dialogue, we must be careful who we share our dreams with. Most people respond in one of two ways. You will find rare gems who support you and tell you to go for it; hang on to those people! You will also uncover some well-meaning folks who let their own fear cast a shadow on your dreams. They will say things like, "You can't quit a good job," Or, "How long are you going to try to make this work before you get a real job?" You will have enough self-doubt; you don't need to listen to that negativity.

Consider the source. People stuck at a job they don't enjoy, living paycheck to paycheck, should not be your guru. Find someone who is successfully on the path where you want to travel and ask them if they regret taking the plunge. Successful people do not let fear and doubt get in their way. Becoming entrepreneurs and controlling our own destinies was one of our best decisions. If we had not jumped in with both feet, we'd have missed out on more than we imagined.

When fear and doubt begin talking, it's easy to let your limiting belief systems kick in. It's vital to remember that what other people think doesn't matter, especially the ones playing it safe. We also must avoid acting on our perceptions of what people might think. We imagine what they will say and allow our behaviors and actions to be skewed. Although, that may have worked in my favor since I set out to prove them wrong. I was determined to show the naysayers that we were not going to fail like they thought we would.

We took a big leap, and to the surprise of almost everyone who knew us, we kicked ass. Within three years, we had replaced both our incomes and paid off the credit cards. We never had to touch the emergency fund, so we returned Tim's mom's loan, too. Growing up, neither of us had much, and we never imagined having more than typical middle-class lives. But six years after we began, we were bringing in more income than either of us had ever dreamed of making.

The special events industry faced challenges following 9/11 and during the Recession of 2008-2012. During the recession, we started a new business, Connections Team

Building Events, to survive the downturn. We recognized that corporations did not have budgets for extravagant summer picnics or holiday parties. They were trying to do more with fewer employees, and their teams needed morale-boosting and bonding experiences to keep going. We filled that need with creative events like Corporate Recess and Scavenger Hunts. And though this began as a way to stay relevant and bring in revenue, the brand has taken on a life of its own.

During this time of growing the business, raising a family, and sacrificing way more to the business than we should have, we experienced some good knocks and dings that provided valuable lessons. One Sunday evening in the middle of May, I was crying on my bathroom floor. I was filthy, sore, exhausted, and had just finished a thirty-two-hour shift. Both Tim and I had worked to set up after-proms and other events with these horribly long hours for five weekends straight.

I was melting down. Life had become way too hard, and I wasn't being the mother I wanted to be. We were making more money than we could have elsewhere and giving our boys opportunities, but we were sacrificing our lives. It wasn't worth this pace.

I planned to tell Tim that I was resigning and was going to get a job. Then I realized I would just get sucked back in. He would need me to just do this one thing or just this one weekend. I thought the only way out would be to pack up the boys and move far away, but that wasn't an option for me. In exhaustion and frustration, I fell asleep. When I woke four hours later, I knew I could not tear apart my family over our business. Aloud I said, "Other people grow companies and do not give up their whole life. We must figure out how to do this better."

We spent the next few years learning how to do it better. I read every book I could, joined mastermind groups, went to start-up conferences, and took classes at the Small Business

Development Center. I was determined to learn how to run a business. I knew there had to be a reason some businesses grow and succeed while others just hobble along until the owners throw up the white flag. I was not ready to wave that flag on the business.

HOPE IS NOT A STRATEGY

One important thing I learned is that hope is not a strategy. You must step away from the business and get some altitude to work *on*, not *in*, the business to create a strategy. I also discovered a ton of tactics, strategic planning, systems, and processes that made entrepreneurship easier—not easy, but easier. I have come to understand the entrepreneurial game has no magic solution; however, some of us make it harder than it should be.

We spent a lot of money on consultants who gave us false hope. They would come in with false promises and say they would fix it for us. I have come to understand that in *our* businesses, *we are the ones who are living it*, so we must be the ones who do the heavy lifting. The trick is to do the lifting in a smarter, not harder, way. That is why we need good coaching rather than fix-it consultants. You need someone to teach you what tools to use and give you an outside perspective while asking you the right questions to dig out the best answers that are inside of you. You need someone who will coach you from the sidelines so that you make the right plays, but *you* must be the one in the game.

In my endeavor to learn how to do things better, I pieced together different parts of each book, class, speaker, and conference that resonated with me. I began with a two-page strategic plan that gave us clarity. We defined who we were and why we did what we did so we could understand our purpose.

We realized that the purpose of our business was to allow others to slow down, enjoy life, and build community. This mission became the rallying cry that gave me a new sense of passion for the business. I originally believed we helped throw parties—which was not really earth-shaking. Understanding the true nature of our impact—the way we helped people laugh, bond, and celebrate special life moments—spoke to my soul.

The work of looking deep into your soul is required to create your Purpose or Mission Statement, whether for your business or for your personal mission, or both. This is the *Why* that Simon Sinek shares in his viral Ted talk from 2009. He later authored the book *Start with the Why*, which dives deep into the idea that without purpose, we will not get the outcome we strive for.

Tim and I had developed a practice of hiring anybody, including friends and family, even if they were not the best suited for the job. Our new business plan gave us clarity on the type of person we needed. We defined what they would be doing and made sure they aligned with our core values. We began hiring only qualified individuals, giving each a list of things they would be responsible for. That list made them excited. I created procedures that made hiring and keeping people easier. We created step-by-step instructions so that the way Tim and I set things up and represented the business was repeatable. We began having meetings to get our team on board with the strategy and passion.

In all of this, I discovered how important a company's culture is. I made sure we never thought of our people as employees or staff. They were our team—our work family. I made it my goal to create an environment that made employees look at their time here as a valuable part of their life, even if they had since moved on. I wanted them to feel as though they had learned something and felt part of something

41

bigger than their job. I explained the concept like this, "I want everyone who leaves here to add us to their Christmas card list and keep us updated on their lives." I wanted them to remember their time with us with fondness.

We have had some incredibly special people work for us, and all are more important than the number of events or the revenue and profit. For some, Fun Pro was their first job, and we've had employees who have gone on to start tech firms that sold for millions, become engineers who design aircraft or become doctors or lawyers.

Several amazing people have chosen a career at Fun Pro. They have been with us for eleven, sixteen, and twenty years. Three couples married because they met while working for us. One of the things I am most proud of when I talk about our entrepreneurial endeavor is the people that have been part of our team and look back positively on the experience.

When we started the business, we were just hoping to make a living and replace our incomes; we never thought about the next steps. We didn't allow ourselves to dream about what could be. The time I spent creating a business plan from a store-bought template and having conversations with dream killers and banks was such a waste. I wish I had known to look for our *"why"* within our strengths and passions. My time would have been better spent defining our dream, determining our values, and planning for smart and intentional growth. We started with the mindset of "Let's see if this will work" as our business strategy. We should have made plans to grow and succeed instead. We may have avoided many growing pains that kicked our butts.

Once you start seeing success in your business, the people around you begin saying things like, "You are so lucky." "It must be great to not have a boss." "You guys get to make all the money and have other people do the work." Just between you, me, and all the other small business owners out there, all these statements are dead wrong!

First, tripping over a winning lottery ticket on the sidewalk is what I would call lucky, and nothing like that ever happened to us. To quote the late Ray Kroc, founder of McDonald's, "Luck is a dividend of sweat. The more you sweat, the luckier you get." Second, I have at least six hundred bosses per year—I call them clients. Third, making money as an entrepreneur can be tricky. There were times when I had my last four paychecks in my purse because the account did not have the funds to cash them after paying everyone else.

Entrepreneurship is not for the weak heart; it takes a certain kind of person and a lot of discipline to be a driven entrepreneur. Becoming the leader and owner of a business means you accept doing the hard things. Entrepreneurs do not get to sit back and wait for someone to reward them for taking the risk. Another mantra I try to remember is *happiness comes when people serve you, but meaning and significance come when you serve others.* That is the goal of leadership.

If I had a dollar or even a dime for every mistake we made in running a business, I wouldn't have to work so hard. The point is to learn from the hard stuff and mistakes, to cherish them as much as the wins—because they make us better. With that in mind, I will take the knocks and learn from them because by doing so, I am getting a lesson in life and leadership.

While stories of resilience can be inspirational, I also want to be honest about how freaking hard it is when you fall before you get up and learn the lesson. I have been encouraged by understanding that our mistakes are sometimes the only things we can truly own. I am grateful for having taken risks and having fallen on my face several times. It is also true that our trials should not be sugar-coated with the beauty of the lessons we find in the emergence.

Please download my E-book titled "My Business Blunders" to get more detailed information on preventing many of the classic business mistakes that we made. My hope is to prevent a few of those dents and dings for you.

TOOLS FOR A JOY-FILLED LIFE

Tool #4

Choose your Circle of Influence Wisely.

Show me your friends, and I'll show you your future.
—Dan Pena

Watch out for dream killers. Be careful how you talk to yourself. Keep an ear out for your limiting beliefs and stories that you tell yourself. When your thoughts turn negative, remind yourself of all you have accomplished and talk to someone who helps you stay positive. I have often reminded myself that if anyone was speaking to my friend, sister, or daughter as I am speaking to myself, I would never tolerate that, so how am I tolerating speaking to myself in this way?

Second, make sure you surround yourself with people who inspire and push you. Talk to driven people who are succeeding in their goals. They have better opinions than those sitting on their couches. I've heard it said you are the sum of the five to ten people you associate with. Darren Hardy quotes Dr. David McClelland of Harvard in *The Compound Effect*, "[the people you habitually associate with] determine as much as 95 percent of your success or failure in life."[5] We are hard enough on ourselves; we doubt, fear, and crush ourselves. We do not need to add fuel to that fire by listening to the naysayers, doubters, and haters.

Step One: Make a list of all those that you spend your time with. Next to each name, write the attributes that you admire about each person. Also, write the things that prove more challenging about each name on your list.

Step Two: Make a list of the attributes you need most in your life.

Step Three: Do the traits from step two match the traits of the people currently in your circle? If not, that doesn't mean you have to cut people from your life. It means you need to seek out some new mentors/friends that will help you be the person you want to be. It also means being aware of how current people in your life are affecting you and create boundaries to not get pulled into thoughts and behaviors that do not serve you well.

Step Four: Draw an arc in the corner of the paper; this is your bubble or sphere of influence. Write the names of the five or ten people whose attributes match your second list, the ones with the attributes you need more of in your life. These should be the people you admire and respect. Those who are living the life you desire. Try to spend your time with these folks.

Step Five: Guard your circle! Maarten van Doorn, a Ph.D. in Philosophy, authored a great article on this topic called "You Are the Average of The Five People You Spend the Most Time With." He states, "The lesson here is to *actively construct* your social environment. Don't let it depend on proximity or chance or on how it has always been, but consciously plan which opinions, attitudes, and life philosophies you do and do not *allow* to be in

your life. These days, people are keen to empha-
size that everyone lives in his or her own bubble.
In that case, we might as well try to make sure
that *our* bubble is the one that rises highest—the
one that makes us reach our goals." [6]

Step Six: A great option for building your community is by
joining mastermind groups. A few of my best
business decisions have been getting involved in
the right communities. I started by joining industry association groups like ILEA (International
Live Events Association) and volunteering for
committees and leadership positions. I learned so
much through my service and developed amazing relationships. I became a member of a CEO
group of six business owners who agreed to meet
monthly and be each other's sounding board and
support. I have also been a long-time member
of the WPO (Women Presidents Organization)
and EO (Entrepreneurs Organization), as well as
Strategic Coach. These groups have been invalu-
able both personally and professionally. I am
continually in awe and feel supported by people
who "get me."

Tool #5

Business Resources

You Need a Plan

We must start and operate our business or our life from a place of purpose, passion, and planning. Abe Lincoln famously said, "Give me six hours to chop down a tree, and I will spend the first four sharpening the ax." You cannot prepare for everything, and most plans have flaws, but you must have a plan; then, you must leap. Clarity on your why will help you get out of bed on those tough days when you are working too hard and not making money. Start with a dream and get crystal clear on where you are going. You can't spend years planning for everything, but when you can see and feel why it matters to you, you will be equipped to rise to fix the challenges that come your way. I am not advocating a 200-page Strategic Plan written for a bank that amortizes the cost of a printer over the next ten years. That type of plan will sit on your shelf gathering dust and will not give you a filter for your direction and day-to-day decision making. I am simply stating the importance of dreaming farther than you can see right now to understand what will get you out of bed when you are exhausted and are barely making ends meet. Business mentor and author Chuck Blakeman shared with me that you must have a plan but advises that every plan will be a bad plan, but you will not know what to fix until you move forward with your plan. The point is to know where you are going and have an idea of how you are going to get there; then move, take action, and fix the plan as you go.

After all the ups and downs of finding a decent life balance, I read *Traction: Get a Grip on Your Business* by Gino Wickman. It was mind-blowing and game-changing—everything I had been trying to do, Mr. Wickman had encapsulated on the pages of his book. His strategy required me and our team to make changes. The book offered no false promises. However, it provided all the tools of Wickman's Entrepreneurial Operating System® (EOS®), which together could solve the key issues in business. This process puts small business owners and their leadership teams in the driver's seat of the business. EOS will give you the tools to create efficiency, organization, and accountability. EOS provides coaches and facilitators to walk you through the journey.

Most teams struggle with dysfunction on some level. Creating a team of individuals who trust one another and act for the greater good is a necessary component of a healthy organization. To this end, my businesses use assessments and training from The Five Behaviors® of a cohesive team modeled after Patrick Lencioni's book *Five Dysfunctions of a Team*. We also use DiSC® Assessments, Kolbe Profiles®, and trust-building activities to ensure the most functional team possible. These allow us to create a circle of internal safety, so our only fight is with the competition. Utilizing these assessments helps you understand yourself and others, making you more effective together. I also like to consider the definition of partnership: an agreement where the parties consent to cooperate to advance their mutual interests. I ask myself, *can I be better, do more, and get further with cooperation than I can alone?* If yes, then the partnership and collaboration with others should come before my own interests.

In our hearts and souls, we wanted to be a place where people felt seen, heard, and understood—a place where they felt they belonged. Profit is always critical in business, but we had a theory that if we put people before profit, the rest would come. One of the best things we did in business was to make culture and employee satisfaction key measurable goals. We created strategies and plans and metrics to measure them. Most importantly, we made them part of the mission.

We increased the P&L category of employee spend by 65%. We raised pay and benefits and added fun bonding events, snacks, and more. We took the employees on an incentive trip to Puerto Vallarta. Not only was it fun, but it felt good. Plus, we saw a 28% gross revenue increase and a 300% profit increase. You can't argue with numbers; they don't lie. A caveat here—you cannot simply throw gifts, money, benefits, and trips at people and hope it makes them work hard to succeed and help grow the company. Everyone must be aligned and have passion for the mission. Team members must also have the ability, desire, training, and experience to be accountable to all roles in their seat, and they must hit goals to reap rewards.

We instituted a pay-for-performance structure and put 10% of the profits into a pot, and assigned points to actions that led to a job well done. If individuals did everything to ensure successful events, happy clients, and profits, it would be reflected in their paychecks. Two books that have fantastic resources around this topic are *Radical Candor*® by Kim Scott and *Why Employees are Always a Bad Idea*® by Chuck Blakeman.

FOUR
IT'S NOT YOUR PLAN

I do not want to foresee the future.
I am concerned with taking care of the present.
God has given me no control over the moment following.
—Mahatma Gandhi

I loved raising kids while running businesses. It allowed flexibility and gave me the ability to prioritize my sons' events and games. There are a lot of joys and pains in being a parent. Nothing pulls your heart and tests your emotions like parenthood. In 2012, our boys were practically grown, and both would be away at college soon. Tim and I finally had the luxury of more free time due to more efficiently running our business. We traveled regularly and started planning for our empty nest future. I would miss having the boys and all their friends around, but thankfully, they both were going to college in-state, so we would see them regularly.

By this time, we had three businesses, and we were considering selling the biggest one. Then each of us would run one of the others. We were excited about focusing on our marriage after twenty-five years together. We could end our business partnership and see what not being together twenty-four/seven looked like.

In October of that year, Josh, our oldest, turned twenty-one. We thought it would be fun to take him and a couple of his friends to Vegas to celebrate. This mother-hen decided to go and keep everyone safe. My dad, both boys, Josh's friend, Tim, and I headed off for a weekend of fun.

While most of the group went off to see the city and its debauchery, seventeen-year-old Hogan and I took in the sights and rode a roller coaster. I had not been feeling well. Tired and nauseated, I thought I might be coming down with something.

LIFE'S LITTLE SURPRISES

Do you remember how it was difficult for me to have children? Our firstborn had been a miracle surprise, and Hogan, our second son, came along three-and-a-half years later with the help of fertility medications. For seven years, we tried to have a third child. As the boys got older, we casually discussed birth control but sort of forgot about it, and though we stopped trying to have another baby, we never started not trying.

When I felt so bad in Vegas, I mentally listed my symptoms. *That's weird; it sounds like pregnancy.* Even though I was sure it was not that, I decided to grab a pregnancy test at the CVS on the Strip, just to be sure. Four positive tests later, I thought, *wow, finding out you're pregnant in Vegas... how cliché! At least we won't need to go to a wedding chapel on the Strip!*

Tim crawled into the hotel bed at about 3:00 a.m. and woke up to me crying at 6:00 a.m. Here we were, at the end of the marathon of parenting... and now we would be starting a new marathon. Tim asked about my tears, and I told him my news.

"Oh shit," He responded. Then he rolled over and went back to sleep. Later that day, when we had another moment alone, he commented again.

"What else were we going to do for the next twenty years?"

"I had a plan. I was going to do a lot," I replied.

We kept it a secret for a while, and I struggled to seem happy. My emotions ran from being shocked to scared to excited to angry. This was not part of my plan. Getting children to adulthood takes everything you've got. Your reward is watching them on their journey while you sit back and enjoy life for a while. I loved being a mom, but if anyone tells you it's pie and ice cream all the time, they are full of it.

Tim was once again all in. He said, "I know you did the heavy lifting with parenting the first two, but I've got you. I will be totally focused on parenting this time around, and you can still make your plans." When we found out we were expecting a girl, he said things like, "She is going to be a daddy's girl. I will be wrapped around her finger, and I am not ashamed to admit it."

My dad said, "You know how this happens, right?" And a friend quoted the old Yiddish proverb, "We plan. God Laughs."

After I recovered from the initial shock, I got excited about our new blessing and had a very spiritual moment. I awoke one morning about three months into my pregnancy and told Tim that this baby was a gift from God. I believed she would cure cancer or lead us to world peace. I shared with him that I felt certain she was a gift for the greater good. I joked that the Virgin Mary and I were both meant to sacrifice for humanity through the birth of our children.

I could never be more thankful for the accidental blessing of my daughter Emmerson Grace. She was born four days before Hogan -our youngest, now middle child's high school graduation.

Raising a child after having done it once is an amazingly fulfilling experience. It is fun watching her grow without the stress of being a first-time parent trying to navigate perfection with no manual. I have learned that the saying, "Children do as we do, not as we say," is absolutely true. So now I work to live the way that I want her to live. I do not mean that I want her to follow my career choices or be a mini-me. I want her to remember that she is perfectly imperfect, custom-designed, and gifted. I live authentically and share my mistakes while I use my gifts so she learns that she can make mistakes and focus on her strengths. She sees that I only have the most important expectations for myself and her. I ask her to be and do her best, and that is all I can ask of myself. Our children are given to us temporarily; they have their own stories and their own lives to navigate. All I can do is love her unconditionally, provide for her, and be my absolute best self as a role model for her.

Emme has dyslexia, ADD, and an incredibly high IQ. It is a distinct joy to see her soak up knowledge—which she learns differently than many. At first, I struggled, wondering how she would cope with her difficulties in school and into adulthood. She taught me that we are all unique and extra struggle is good; it creates grit.

My sons had an easy time in school; they put in minimal effort and made good grades. So, when faced with a struggle, it is hard for them to deal with it. Emme's resilience and striving over adversity will serve her well. She has taught me so much more than I can teach her. Emmerson is extremely empathetic and has huge feelings; I need a bit more of that in my life.

My daughter is a much better advocate for herself than I ever was for myself. One day, I was helping her read with mild frustration.

"This word is 'their,'" I said. "You just read that in the last sentence."

"I forget. It takes me time to figure it out. If I gave you a music sheet, you couldn't read that, but I can play the piano with it. We all have things we are better at."

How about that for a life lesson? One of the greatest things about Emme is that she has about 100% of Tim Abbott's DNA. She looks like him, talks like him, gestures and moves like him, so we all get to see a bit of him daily. I feel excited about how differently-abled she is. I am inspired by the amazing fortitude and accomplishments of folks who are dyslexic: Richard Branson, Walt Disney, Albert Einstein, John F. Kennedy, George Washington, John Lennon, and Pablo Picasso, not to mention several personal friends, mentors, and people I respect highly. Many of these people credit the way their minds work with their ability to achieve. They all said growing up in a world that teaches all people in only one way gave them the grit and tenacity they needed to overcome life's challenges.

All I know is that if you had asked me what I would be doing after my sons went off to college, I never would have answered, "I think I will raise another child." I am thankful that I am not in control of making all the plans because this option is better than any plan I had dreamed up. My life is a constant reminder that I am not in control all of the time. Every time I think I have everything under control, I get a big thump on the forehead that knocks me off my pedestal, reminding me to let go and realize that I do not have to figure it all out on my own. I am reminded that I can pray for what I want, but sometimes the prayers will be answered with what I need instead.

TOOLS FOR A JOY-FILLED LIFE

Tool #6

Let Go of Control

Make plans, strive to be your best, and pray for what you want, but remember, life doesn't always happen according to your plan. This may seem counter to the locus of control concept, but here is the difference: by taking responsibility for what occurs in your life, you can make changes as needed if things are not working for you. By thinking that you must control everything or that you make all the decisions, you are going to be disappointed. In her blog post, *How to Let Go of Control: 8 No Nonsense Tips*, Catherine Winter says, "Control serves little real purpose. It's a process of confirmation bias. That is, we think we're in control when one of the plans we made comes to fruition as we planned it. We considered it, we planned it, and everything went as planned. What about all the times that things didn't go as planned? How much weight do we give to those plans that went awry for whatever reason? Sometimes they go wrong because of what you did or didn't do. Other times it's because of circumstances far out of your control. To let go of control doesn't mean you stop planning or stop trying to do things. Instead, letting go of control is about releasing the fear and anxiety that causes us to cling to what we think we know."[7]

An article in *Fast Company* provides a lot of helpful information on mindfulness techniques for letting go of control. Anisa Purbasari Horton writes, "We tend to ask questions and generate 'what-ifs' as an attempt to introduce some certainty when we're uncomfortable with the unknown. But as psychologist Simon Rego told Stephanie Vozza, a more mindful way to approach this is to build tolerance for uncertainty. Then, you can slowly identify which of your worries are 'useful' and which are making you 'unnecessarily miserable.' You can choose to let go of the latter and prepare 'strategic solutions' for the former."[8]

I use a mantra with hand gestures—mine (while patting my chest), theirs (while pointing outwardly), and His (while pointing up)—to help me remember I can only control what is mine. I try to keep my worry container small. We can easily start worrying about more than what is ours to worry about. We start with everything in our own home and family and just keep adding things to worry about. We fret about our neighbors, friends, community, and world until the stress becomes unbearable. I like to keep in mind that I only have the capacity to carry the stress and worry that fit in the small basket on my desk. I can't let myself choose a giant dumpster-size worry and stress container because the visual helps me filter out the things I cannot control.

FIVE
LIFE QUAKE

You don't know who is important to you
until you actually lose them.
—Mahatma Gandhi

In May of 2013, our little surprise blessing made her debut, and we let our beautiful baby girl monopolize our time. Our younger son Hogan would be going to Colorado University in Boulder at the end of August, and Josh would be returning to Colorado State University, so we took our annual family trip to Lake Powell. The trip was wonderful. Tim played hard—his need for speed was a regular topic of conversation, laughter, and sometimes fear and annoyance on my part. He did nothing halfway, which meant I witnessed him doing crazy things that scared me. Boating, skiing, and deep-sea diving were three of his passions. I enjoyed them with him at a much slower pace. When we skied, he went ten times faster than my speed, doing trick jumps and screaming past me. On the lake, I floated around, soaking up the sun, or drove the boat while he and the kids flipped and did tricks behind the watercraft on wakeboards. I enjoyed calm ocean dives at thirty to forty feet while Tim dove into caves and shipwrecks, going as deep as the water pressure allowed. We were a good mix—he pushed me and challenged my need for calm stability, and I reminded him to be careful.

On one of the days of our Lake Powell vacation, Tim jumped off a fifty-foot cliff into the water. He rode a jet ski at sixty miles per hour and a wakeboard with all the kids our sons' ages. Only two weeks from his fiftieth birthday, he was strong and lived life with a zest most people can never imagine.

That August evening, the 100-degree temperatures had our group decide to get into the lake to cool off before bed. Not even the moon offered any light when Tim used the water slide for his entry into the cool water. I was changing into a swimsuit inside the boat's cabin when a massive thud knocked me off balance. With my heart racing, I ran to see what had happened.

Everyone was in a panic. Tim, in adrenaline-junkie fashion, went down the water slide on his feet. There is certainly no fun or challenge in taking a waterslide on your butt, right? The group witnessed his banana-peel-style fall. His head hitting the edge of the boat had caused the jolt. When he entered the water, he was unconscious. When Tim did not resurface, panic struck.

Dive after dive produced no results. We couldn't find my husband in the dark water. For the next few hours, I huddled with my three-month-old baby and prayed. That was the longest night of my life. With every noise, I jumped to see if it was Tim. The shock wouldn't give way to the pain of losing him. I kept thinking he had climbed onto a rock somewhere, waiting for rescuers. Tim was like Superman; a water slide could never take him out!

The next day, divers recovered his body at sixty-seven feet underwater. I lay on his chest and felt my whole life stand still. I had counted on this man for twenty-five years, and I couldn't make it without him. How could this be happening? We would never be the same.

As I lay there, I didn't think I could ever get up again. And then I heard my daughter cry. She needed food, and I had to get up and keep living. I couldn't give up; my kids needed a sane mother.

RECOVERING FROM THE QUAKE

Grief is a tricky thing that is part of the human experience. Most of us will not get through life without experiencing some grief. For many, it will be losing a loved one, but we can also grieve the loss of a job or marriage. We can grieve the end of a relationship or a project we loved. Counselors tell us that to maneuver through grief, one must simply do the next right thing. That might be getting a drink of water or brushing your teeth. Thinking about the future is too difficult.

The next right thing for me was keeping my baby alive. I had to hold and feed a fussy baby, change her diaper, then put her down for a nap. Day after day, I repeated the simple tasks. I had to be strong for this little girl. She no longer had to save the world; she was here to save me. I clung to her. My baby's need for me meant my survival. I realized that, once again, God had a plan. It was Tim's time to leave this world, but God had given me the gift of Emme before taking him.

It was lonely. The boys were at college, and I was in a big house with a baby who didn't speak or interact. I had friends and family for support, but I sat alone often. I could've filled those hours with TV, classes, girl's nights, movies, and more. But I had a baby who needed her mom. It gave me lots of time to think. I had never stopped for long enough to realize I had an addiction to busyness; I had just rolled with it for the last twenty-five years.

I believe you cannot fully grieve with people always around you, and you cannot get through it completely alone. Sometimes, my house felt so empty and lonely, despite being with my baby. While this gave me room to scream, cry, and pray, I am forever grateful for friends and family who came to spend time with me or have sleepovers.

Bruce Feiler, author of *Life is in the Transitions,* coined the phrase Life Quake. He describes it as "a massive life change that is high on the Richter scale of consequences and has aftershocks for years."[9] He wrote the book because, as he states, he "had a huge life quake, a period of wrenching personal change when crises seemed to be piling up. For many years, I enjoyed what I now call a linear life, conventional success, marriage, and family." He further says, "We are primed to expect that our lives will follow a predictable path, and we're thrown when they don't. We have linear expectations but nonlinear realities."

Someone once shared with me the idea that if money can fix the problem, it is not really a problem. That insight adds perspective. Losing a loved one, compromised health, and damaged integrity are true losses that money can't fix.

In grief, everything balances on a continuum, like many parts of our lives. We must take note of our actions and even more important is to know our purpose for those actions. Am I over-functioning or under-functioning, staying too busy with people or isolating myself, ignoring self-care, or focusing on being a victim? It is a rough road to remain in the healthy middle because extremes can put you over the edge.

With a traumatic loss comes secondary losses. While I lost my spouse, my business partner, and the father of my children, I also lost my best friend, handyman, lawn guy, car guy, date to functions, and my partner in life. This meant bouts of grief popped up whenever I had to do almost anything on my own. I've always been very independent and took care of things myself in the past. Now, suddenly, I felt helplessness and waves of sadness when I had to shovel snow or go to a business function by myself. I had done those things hundreds of times on my own before Tim died. Now it was different.

The other thing I noticed was a loss of identity. Since I was no longer Tim's wife, it felt as if we were no longer the Abbotts. Who was I if I wasn't who I had been for the last two-and-a-half decades? There were times I found myself taking on a new identity that would have kept me stuck in grief if I didn't choose to change it. At first, I embraced the identity of the widow and the sad victim of life's circumstances. And I am grateful I had my kids to keep me going and the businesses to push me to stay awake and abandon those temporary identities. I had to decide that I wanted to live and feel joy again, and that work helped me to feel okay and continue.

While grief is a journey that I would not wish on anyone, it taught me a lot. Pain is where God shouts. It made me appreciate those I love in a whole new way. It gave me new perspectives. For instance, the only thing that is life or death is life or death. I learned to ask myself, *will this really matter in twenty years?* Grief is not linear, it is unorganized, and it is not the same for any two people. It is a hot mess; you have a lot of doubts and a myriad of emotions. I faced denial, anger, guilt, bargaining, depression, plus several other phases of grief, but from my experience, they are not linear stages. They are an enormous balls of yarn, tangled, interwoven, and jumbled. If you try to pinpoint how you feel, you'll go crazy because sometimes, you feel several distinct emotions at once, and other times, it is a woven mess of emotions that turns into a whole new feeling. It is a scary, lonely, and rocky road. Sometimes I walked in a complete fog; I have no recollection of several things that happened during those first months. Sometimes I felt guilty in moments of joy. How could I be laughing when Tim died? Other times I forgot he was gone, and I would call him. There is a list a mile long of normal grief experiences. Things I would never have imagined feeling or doing surfaced. If you are dealing with loss, know that you are not crazy, even if it feels like it. There is no right or perfect way to grieve.

Grief is tough on all your relationships. Well-meaning people will try to be comforting but say things that sting. Others do not know what to say, so they avoid you. Now when I hear of someone's loss, I just show up and say, "I am so sorry for your loss and pain. I have nothing to say that will fix this, but I am thinking about you and praying for your peace." That is all you need to do to be there for a friend, and it helps!

LIFE AFTER THE QUAKE

We give ourselves and others a gift when we extend a helping hand or ask others to help us. As humans, we feel significant and part of the tribe when we give of ourselves. It relieves some of our grief.

Facilitating GriefShare groups is one of the best things I have done for myself since Tim's death. Helping others through their grief journeys has given purpose to my loss. Being a light to show others they can get through the pain has blessed me. I show them what the future can look like when they get to the other side of the quake and do the grief work. And they get to see the hope of joy again if they do the work. These groups and the program have taught me so much about the grief journey. Number one—it is a journey that requires goal setting, making choices, and doing some of the hard things that you might rather avoid.

I have discovered untrue clichés and beliefs, such as "time heals." If you sit around and wait for time to go by, thinking someday you will wake up feeling better, you will be disappointed. You actually have to do the work to heal. The sting of acute grief fades over time but choosing to set goals and choosing the life you want is how you heal, not by waiting for time to pass. Also, you might think you can't live without your loved one, but you have everything you need to be alive. Some people feel robbed—that God, the universe, someone, or something stole or took their loved ones from them. The truth is our loved ones never belonged to us—everyone we love is ours on loan.

Grief work also includes concrete things, such as journaling, seeking therapy, joining a group, and writing a grief letter. Less tangible is the daily choice to get up and live. When a monsoon of grief hits, I deal with it and take care of myself. I had a habit of asking myself each day if I felt well enough to function out in the world. One day, I intentionally stopped asking myself how I felt, and instead, I got up and assumed I was okay until I found out otherwise. That was powerful because if I allowed my feelings to drive my answer, I would, of course, be miserable, in despair, and too sad to live. Even when not grieving, we can use this strategy of getting up and choosing to feel good; we simply choose happy. Also, we understand that when we get hit with hard emotions, we must allow ourselves to feel them. Lastly, we might believe that life will return to what it was, to normal. You will one day feel joy, love, hope, and peace again, but life and who you are will never be exactly as it was; you will have a new and different normal. But new and different does not have to mean bad.

More major growth occurred in those few years after Tim's death than in my first forty-four years of life. I had an overwhelming feeling that Tim was one of the good guys who got to go to Heaven while I had to stay here in Earth school to grow into my higher purpose and make the impact God intended me to make. Without that loss, I would never have become all I was created to be. When I had my titles of wife, business partner, and mother, I was not looking for what else I was supposed to do. As I came out of the fog of acute grief with altered titles, I got new, valuable life lessons.

First, I learned to walk in the light of gratitude. I spent so much of my life seeing what was wrong and not what was right. Before my loss, I looked at what I needed to improve to be happy, such as things in my marriage and job. I focused on what I didn't have and my mile-long to-do list instead of all the amazing blessings I had.

When I lost Tim, I could only remember the good things about him and our life together. I missed all those wonderful things, and I hated knowing that I would never have them again. Why didn't I appreciate them more at the time? Why did I take it all for granted while I had it? Now, I will never stop living in the light of gratitude and never stop feeling a deep appreciation for my blessings. When I lose anything or anyone in my life, I will not have taken them for granted. What you look at is what you see. I choose to look at the good. Today, go out and look for the good, hug your people, and consider all you would miss if they were not here. Choose to avoid the enemy of gratitude—focusing on what you *don't* have. The next time you trip over those shoes in the hallway, think about how you would feel if they were gone.

Next, I realized I have more control over my emotions than I knew. We look at the circumstances that are out of our control and say, "When I fix that, or when I get this or meet that, then I will be happy." I assure you, unless you make a conscious choice to be happy right now, regardless of your circumstances, you will not be happy. Tim worked hard and played hard, and he mostly chose happiness. I would completely dishonor his legacy if I chose misery every day. To think his passing caused any of his loved ones to wallow in sadness and not live fully with intention would horrify him.

Even when things aren't going well, I get up every day and *choose* happiness. While I may not be Suzy Sunshine every minute, if I face a struggle, I will fare better with a positive state of mind than a negative one. I embrace the good, bad, and ugly experiences because all of them will get me to my highest and best. My emotions are mine, and I get to choose them. My experiences, situations, the surrounding people, my job, car, and house do not control my emotions—*I do!* Choose gratitude; what happens might surprise you.

WHAT ABOUT THE AFTERSHOCKS?

Feelings happen. No one is immune. For a while, I worried that if I let the grief have its way, they would have to scrape me off the floor and into a mental ward. I thought if I stopped to feel, I would never get started again.

One day, my therapist asked how I was dealing with the hard feelings.

"I need to be strong for my family and staff," I said,

"What is strong?" she asked.

"Strong is a rock or a mountain, something that can withstand and be counted on."

"What if you could be strong like clay instead?"

The epiphany engulfed me. If I were clay, I could smoosh into a puddle of nothing if I needed to. I could roll up in a ball and cry or be a puddle on the floor and just lose it for a while. Then I could transform into a mountain again and not worry about falling apart and never being whole again. I was stronger than a rock! As clay, I could choose to crumble any time I needed; then, I could rebuild the way I wanted. The clay analogy freed me to feel what I needed to feel and then wash my face and go out into the world again. Even beyond grief, this analogy still helps me to feel the emotions and know I will get through it.

People smarter than me said, "Be a screen, not a door." And my perspective changed some more. A screen could let the feelings of sadness, grief, loss, anger, resentment, loneliness, and unfairness wash through me. They could enter, fill every fiber of my being, teach me what I needed to learn, and then help me heal and create an impact from my pain. A screen allowed them to go right on through when they finished. I traded in my door that shut them out or kept them in. I would let those feelings blow through on the breeze.

Through all those greenhouses of growth and a bunch of people supporting me, I took my blown-wide-open self and examined every piece. For the first time, I got to know myself and learned everything I could on my own. Then I found people placed in my path to help me know myself even better. I learned about my strengths, character, flaws, and beliefs. I learned about the things I wanted to improve and the things I needed to capitalize on. I awakened to find a place of passion and purpose. Knowing the why of my existence is powerful. When you know who you are, why you exist, and what your vision and passions are, life is purposeful, bold, and joyful! You can live fully with meaning and intention. I will never go through the motions and live according to the expected to-do list again. Instead, I will live on purpose and live boldly, allowing myself to be afraid and uncomfortable so I don't miss the best parts of life. I will push my limits, believe in myself, and give it all to God. You can, too!

One blessing of my new reality is my understanding that life is fair. Why do we ask, "Why me?" A much better query is, "Why not me?" Pain and struggles will come, as will beauty and blessings. Whether you feel low or are riding high, say, "Life is fair, and why not me?" You get much better answers with the right questions and the proper perspective. Several times after Tim died, I would say, "Life is fair." People looked at me oddly. Most couldn't fathom how life being cut short at forty-nine with a new baby is fair. For people of faith, grieving a lost loved one is not usually about being sad for them. My beloved Tim is in a better place, with no pain or despair. I grieve because of what I lost; I miss him in all life's experiences, and I miss talking to him when I need him. What I am missing is the reason I grieve. I have had so many blessings; it makes sense I would have some struggles as well. Grief is a gift that only comes because we enjoyed one of the greatest gifts—the gift of loving someone. That is fair. Life is fair. We all get some good and some bad. Every blessing and every struggle are opportunities to grow. God doesn't offer a transactional relationship. Going to church and doing the right things doesn't keep the bad away. It just doesn't work that way, I am afraid. The difficulties are as much a gift as the blessings, and both are part of the human experience given to us to help us grow.

TOOLS FOR A JOY-FILLED LIFE

Tool #7

Gratitude and Feeling the Emotions

There are many resources for starting or improving your practice of gratitude and doing so will make amazing improvements to your life. In an interview for The Global Leadership Summit, Brené Brown states, "The relationship between joy and gratitude was one of the important things I found in my research. I wasn't expecting it. In my twelve years of research on eleven thousand pieces of data, I did not interview one person who had described themselves as joyful, who also did not actively practice gratitude. For me, it was very counterintuitive because I went into the research thinking that the relationship between joy and gratitude was: if you are joyful, you should be grateful. But it wasn't that way at all. Instead, practicing gratitude invites joy into our lives."[10]

There are great gratitude practices available. Some of my favorites are gratitude journaling, writing thank-you notes, counting your blessings daily, praying, and meditating. I enjoy starting my day by being grateful for waking up. Then ending the day by listing what I am grateful for that day. Search the internet for "gratitude practices" to find more.

A recent Harvard Medical School article researched the scientifically proven benefits of gratitude. They reported the following results: "In positive psychology research, gratitude is strongly and consistently associated with greater happiness. Gratitude helps people feel more positive emotions, relish good experiences, improve their health, deal with adversity, and build strong relationships."[11]

Gratitude can even affect your business. Statistics show that employees who experience more gratitude at work report fewer depressive symptoms and stress. Ninety-five percent of employees agree that a grateful boss is more likely to be successful. Also, 70% of employees would feel better about themselves, and 81% would work harder if their boss were more grateful. Finally, regular gratitude journaling has resulted in a 5%–15% increase in optimism and a 25% increase in sleep quality.[12]

Here is a fun little activity that I use when I feel my focus needs adjustment. I put ten pennies in my left pocket. When I see something that makes me feel grateful, I move a penny from my left pocket into my right pocket. The mission is to end the day with all ten pennies in my right pocket. The practice allows us to look intentionally for the good in our lives.

One day I was feeling especially sorry for myself, and I didn't know how I could move forward. But I had to move pennies. When I tripped on a curb and almost fell, I thought,

Phew, that would have sucked to fall in the street and rip my pants and scrape my knee. I realized that was enough gratitude to move a penny today. It's amazing what a shift in perspective will do.

Another new perspective is to choose happiness. A great resource for practices in choosing happiness is Marc and Angel Chernoff's book *1000+ Little Things Happy, Successful People Do Differently*. They wrote, "Happiness is a choice. For every minute you are angry or irritated, you lose sixty seconds of happiness. Be happy. Be yourself. If others don't like it, then let them be. Life isn't about pleasing everybody. If you have the courage to admit when you're scared, the ability to laugh even as you cry, the nerve to speak up even if your voice is shaking, the confidence to ask for help when you need it, and the wisdom to take it when it's offered, then you have everything you need to get yourself to a happier state of mind."[13]

While choosing happiness is my jam, I also choose to examine all the other emotions and feel them as I need to. This demonstrates the be-a-screen-not-a-door concept. Our emotions guide us to see what we need and how we can grow. It is important to let them all in, discerning how, why, and what you need to learn from what you are feeling. I recommend the book by Dr. Susan David, Ph.D., *Emotional Agility*. She wants to help people get unstuck, embrace change, and thrive in work and life and says we must examine our feelings since they will drive our actions, careers, relationships, happiness, and health.[14]

I feel joy again. I can think of Tim and embrace all the memories and fun instead of falling apart. My loss will color every special moment for the rest of my life. In each beautiful time of life—marriage, holidays, business milestones, and successes—my family feels joy, but we also feel the hole left by Tim's absence. We must understand pain and peace can coexist. In her book, *When Your Soul Aches: Hope and Help for*

Women Who Have Lost Their Husbands, Lois Mowday Rabey says if we think we must feel the pain no longer to know we are at peace, we will never actually be at peace because the pain may be there forever, in smaller amounts. Pain will always have a place in life here on Earth.[15] I find so much solace in all areas of my life from understanding that pain and peace can coexist. This means we do not have to have everything figured out to find peace. We can be anxious or sad, we can screw up, and we can still have peace.

SIX
FINDING YOURSELF

Our deepest fear is not that we are inadequate. Our deepest fear is that we are powerful beyond measure. It is our light, not our darkness that most frightens us. We ask ourselves, 'Who am I to be brilliant, gorgeous, talented, fabulous?' Actually, who are you not to be? You are a child of God. Your playing small does not serve the world. There is nothing enlightened about shrinking so that other people won't feel insecure around you. We are all meant to shine, as children do. We were born to make manifest the glory of God that is within us. It's not just in some of us; it's in everyone. And as we let our own light shine, we unconsciously give other people permission to do the same. As we are liberated from our own fear, our presence automatically liberates others.

—Marianne Williamson, *A Return to Love*

My big life quake brought many changes to the business. Before, even with all the processes and procedures giving us some life balance, unfortunately, I lived as a control freak, inserting myself into every process and system. Afraid to let go, I needed to be a part of all the decisions. No one else could do it quite right. I couldn't give up my best clients, no matter how the qualified team wanted to help us grow. It fed my ego to be needed. Though I enjoyed the balance and freedom, I created a lot of clogging and hassles for the team. I enjoyed my time away, but while I was away, people at the office waited for my return so they could be productive. My time off generally included returning emails and answering calls rather than playing with my family.

August and September are busy times for events in Colorado. After we lost Tim, I did not have the capacity to care about the business. I was physically unable to care about events, tasks, and decisions. I had one thought: *I can't do this alone, and I need to sell immediately.*

Fortunately, our business was smart and healthy. We had a smart strategy, financial acumen, systems, and marketing. We also had a healthy team and work culture that I never gave enough credence to, but during this tragic time, my competent Fun Pro team rallied around, picked up the ball, and ran with it. Though reeling from the loss and full of uncertainty and fear themselves, they kept trucking and made sure things ran smoothly.

THEY DIDN'T NEED ME

The businesses operated smoothly without me inserting myself into every decision. I was able to remove my ego and loosen control to empower my team. I realized I am passionate about helping people, discovering their strengths, and building teams around engaged individuals. Part of growing a business requires a major mindset shift at a certain stage. As the book *Traction*™ says, you must let go of the vine and Delegate and Elevate™ others to break through the ceiling. You cannot scale without creating more versions of yourself and your teams.

In addition to the personal internal remodeling, the gift of trauma forced me to let go and empower my team. My business had become the vehicle for the life I wanted and gave people a place to work where they are seen, understood, and their strengths and passions can be utilized. I was sure I could not run the business by myself, but then I realized I was never alone. I had a whole team of people with me. I realized that had always been true; I just hadn't let myself notice.

Once I realized how little the day-to-day operations needed me, I began the full-time job of self-discovery. I became intentional about how I wanted to live the rest of my life. I did not want to just roll with it. I wanted to figure out who I was, what I was good at, what I loved to do, where I was going, and how I would get there. I realized that I had decisions to make about my future, and I wanted to have some filters for making those decisions, so as I worked on figuring out my true self, I wrote what became *My Map of Me*, a guide to living intentionally. Please use the QR in the Appendix section at the back of this book to download a copy of your own personal Map of Me.

I took classes and workshops, read books, used assessments, and generally found all the resources I could to dig into why I was put on this earth. I found books like *Quiet* by Susan Cain that gave me permission to be my introverted self, and I no longer felt the need to "be more outgoing." I could lead in my introspective way and not beat myself up for what I wasn't. We are all uniquely gifted, and when people discover and use their gifts to serve their true purpose, it is magical. The world could miss out on what you can bring when you merely go to work and live life without passion. We lack the feeling of significance when we do not live and use our greatness by knowing ourselves.

It starts early in children. When a child does not fit in the box of the average learner, the schools and parents spend time and money shoring up the places where the student does not measure up. What if we diverted that energy to art, music, running, or writing coaches to reinforce the things the children love and at which they excel? I know kids need to learn math and reading; however, if we all focused on our giftedness, we could be at our best and serve this world beautifully, as we have been designed to do.

THE NEW ME

It was in the messy middle of my self-discovery that I got a few certifications. The best part about becoming certified in DiSC° personality assessments, The Five Behaviors of a Cohesive Team°, PAX Understanding Women° and Understanding Men°, and EOS is that I could try it all at my own companies. I learned two things about these tools.

First, they work! These tools help individuals understand themselves, understand others, and work to bridge the gap to be more effective in all their interactions. Second, I found my calling, purpose, and passion. I began to understand that special events were Tim's passion. On the other hand, I loved creating teams, cultures, systems, and efficiencies. Tim was 100% visionary, while I am 72 Visionary™ and 66 Integrator™. Tim had twenty or more new ideas every day, including innovations and visions for the future of our business. However, he did not enjoy dealing with details and getting in the weeds to bring the ideas to fruition. So, I stepped into that role and dealt with the day-to-day details. I had to improve my skills at being an Integrator to serve that role for all those years we ran the company together.

Rocket Fuel™ by Gino Wickman and Mark Winters helped me better understand visionaries and integrators. I realized I wanted to help other business owners with their teams, cultures, and efficiencies. My new passion was coaching others to grow their businesses with fewer mistakes and a shorter learning curve. I was not sure what that would look like. Although I had determined the *why* and *what* of my future, the *how* was still a bit iffy.

Working with companies to build stronger teams that are more fun and more effective became one of my ambitions. I knew I could help them reach collective goals through those assessments and workshops. Small businesses and entrepreneurs should be able to do good in the world without all the stress and sacrifice. They have the most potential to impact the world. Successful businesses improve families, communities, and lives. My experiences in life and business made it clear—I was meant to be a small business coach. I am passionate about helping entrepreneurs live their lives and not sacrifice them for their businesses. Acutely aware of how everything can be lost in the blink of an eye, I want leaders to enjoy the life they have by using their businesses as the engines for living their best.

During my time of self-discovery, I went back and forth about whether or not I would sell Fun Productions. In 2017, Josh, my oldest son, then twenty-five, told me he wanted to take over and buy the company someday. I was worried about the statistics and downfalls of second-generation businesses. According to a Johnson Cornell College of Business report from BusinessWeek 2010, forty percent of businesses turn into second-generation businesses. Only approximately 13% are passed down successfully to a third generation, and 3% to a fourth generation or beyond.[16] I have heard the reason is that most second-generation owners never had the hard-knock lessons or had to wear all the hats in the business, so they lack that experience. When Josh addressed his desire, I had just read *Traction*, and I knew that the Entrepreneurial Operating System (EOS) and its Proven Process would be the right choice for Josh and me to navigate this transition.

I wanted the vision for the future of the company to be *his* vision. Every new system, process, meeting, and tool needed to be his, not mine. During the transition phase, the cohesive, healthy team had to be *his* team.

Through implementing The EOS Process®, 2017-2019 proved to be the company's best years ever. We increased gross revenue by 30% and net profit by 300% and had a ton of fun doing it. I worried less about Josh taking over, and I knew it was time for me to move on to fulfill my purpose. EOS made sure Josh was set up for future success. I knew he would be fine in taking the business to the next level.

Seeing the value in the process allowed me to choose a career for the next phase of my life. I have become a Professional EOS Implementer®. I believe it is the most simplified and effective system and set of tools to create strategic growth for small businesses. I love helping small business owners get what they want from their companies. We work together to clarify their vision, put strategies and tools in place, and create an empowered team as the fuel to get them there.

TOOLS FOR A JOY-FILLED LIFE

Tool #8

The Map of Me

The government and insurance companies have assigned a value to human life. It turns out that a human would be worth about $10 million on the stock exchange. Unfortunately, we sometimes ask the wrong person about our worth and get the wrong answer. The person in the mirror might lowball the number.

To find your worth a bit faster than I did, I encourage you to get "The Map of Me" (please see the appendix for a link). This resource will help you to:

Find useful tools and assessments
Create a vision for your life
Discover and align with your values
Declare your BHAG (Big, Hairy, Audacious Goal)
Uncover your innate gifts
Create a filter to help you be intentional and make the best decisions for your life

SEVEN
A NEW ADVENTURE AWAITS

If you want to lift yourself up, lift up someone else.
—Booker T. Washington

That first year after Tim's death, I chose to spend many of the holidays and milestones entirely differently from how we had spent them historically in the Abbott house. I thought Thanksgiving and Christmas would be too painful if we kept our traditions without Tim. I rented a beach house and invited my whole family. Another time, we spent the holiday with a family member we had never celebrated with before. I thought if everything were vastly different, it might not feel so different, whereas a traditional celebration would make it glaringly obvious something was amiss.

The first Easter following Tim's death, my family came to my house to celebrate. My two younger sisters were lying on the floor with their phones and laughing. When I asked what was so funny, they were coy and evasive, but I was insistent. They introduced me to online dating apps. I told them it sounded like choosing a partner from a catalog and dismissed it as ridiculous. The conversation moved to how fun and interesting it could be for the three of us to draft a book about dating. At that time, I was a forty-five-year-old widow with a baby and two grown children, my middle sister was a thirty-eight-year-old divorcee raising two young children, and our baby sister was a thirty-year-old who had never been married. We could write about dating in the modern world from these three very different perspectives and ages. To spare anyone's embarrassment, we would not use anyone's names; we would only share some stories of our experiences. As our idea took form, I started online dating as a research project, but I would not *really* date. I was not ready for that.

NOT REALLY DATING

I realized I had never dated as an adult. I was only eighteen when I met Tim, and I decided now was the time to sow some wild oats, all in the name of authoring a book with my sisters. But I made some rules for myself:

1. Don't date while breastfeeding. I waited until Emme was a year old and weaned to start the online version of the dating game.
2. Keep it casual. I was not going to have another marriage or partner. The dating would not even be real.
3. Do not hurt anyone or lead them on. I would certainly never get attached.

On the first date of my adult life, I went to a basketball game. Unbelievably, I saw my oldest son and his girlfriend on the jumbotron. They were at the same basketball game. I clearly hadn't thought this through. I was not ready to run into people I knew while on a date, especially my son. So, I decided I should go public with the fact that I was dating. However, I told everyone they would never meet anyone I was seeing. I would never get married, and the kids would never have another father.

I met some interesting people and had a lot of awkward, annoying, and soul-searching times during that phase. You do learn a lot about yourself through interacting with others; that part was good. However, dating started to become an unhealthy game for me at some point. It became like playing Candy Crush. Just like a dumb phone game, you know you should be doing something else, and this is wasting your time. Yet, you just keep hitting play again. It was like any other distraction or procrastination—fun for a bit and often regretful afterward.

Four months into this game of dating, I decided to call it quits. I had learned a wealth of information about myself. I decided I would dedicate the next year to the self-discovery I had started, and I would reconsider this little social oat-sowing thing again in a year or so.

But I still had one last date on my calendar. I told myself I should just cancel, but I hate conflict or causing any hurt feelings.

THE LAST DATE

This date started a bit differently from the others. To begin with, because I had decided this was my last date, I had no expectations. I was completely myself because I didn't really care if he liked me or if he wanted to see me again. Dr. Chris Donaghue, a therapist and author, says it best: "Date to be known, not to be liked." Apparently, that has a lot of merit because that was my unintentional attitude when I showed up at Starbucks to meet Darren Davis for coffee.

Four hours later, I was still at Starbucks, being totally real and vulnerable, when he asked me for a second date. I said yes, not because I didn't know how to say no, but because I really wanted to see him again. I had shared my story and a lot of my flaws, and he did too; it was refreshing. We spent most of our free time together over the next couple of months as friends.

Darren had been adopted by his stepfather, whom he adored and respected. He had four grown children, did not drink, smoke, or do drugs, and was a faithful man. He was professionally successful, and he was hot!

There were a couple of problems: number one, I was breaking my rules, and number two, I did not think he was physically attracted to me. He never tried to hold my hand or kiss me for two whole months. While hiking one day, he revealed his feelings for me.

"I see us being in each other's lives forever, whatever that looks like, even if just friends." At that moment, I realized I did not want to be his friend; I was falling in love with him. Tears ran down my face.

"I am sorry; I think this is over. I do not want to be your friend, and I understand that you are not attracted to me."

He replied with an amazing kiss! He explained that he was trying to be respectful. He was afraid he would hurt me after I had been with one man for twenty-five years, but attraction was not the issue.

What was supposed to be a fifteen-minute meeting for coffee that was to be the last date of an experiment had turned into hours of profound, deep conversation. How could I be so fortunate to get two soulmates? I have no idea, but life *is* fair. I have done nothing to deserve this, but God blessed me nonetheless. I say it a lot—we pray for what we want and plan our life accordingly, but we end up getting what we need.

> LOVE IS WHAT YOU FIND WHEN YOU STOP SEARCHING AND INSTEAD FOCUS ON BECOMING THE BEST YOU THAT YOU CAN BE.
>
> —CHARLES ORLANDO, RELATIONSHIP EXPERT

I found a man that was everything I needed in a partner—a man who helps me fulfill my journey. He carried all the characteristics that would allow me to get through my limiting beliefs, free my inner child, and count on someone besides myself. I offered what he had been lacking as well.

I can remember watching couples who seemed way too perfect to be real. I spent too much time judging them. Clearly, being able to imagine walking in others' shoes was not part of my personality in the before times. I have come to discover that empathy brings more understanding and joy to life.

As I contemplated my beautiful, passionate, God-arranged relationship, I worried it was too soon and wondered what people would think. I judged myself and, therefore, feared judgment. Through prayer and meditation, I received clarity. I realized I was not doing anything wrong. Loving someone and bringing love into my family should not be judged harshly. From that moment, I vowed to live and let live. I try to respect others for their uniqueness and let go of any notion that my way is the right way. After all, it is none of my business what others think of me. Nor is it my place to judge others and their choices.

THE NEW ADVENTURE

We got married in a tree house all by ourselves a year later. Because Darren was adopted, he had always considered adopting. Darren adopted Emmerson Grace, and she officially became an Abbott-Davis with a daddy who loves her. If asked about her two last names, she says, "I have two dads, so I get two last names." My boys are blessed with a positive role model and a friend. I have gained four adult stepchildren who add joy, complexity, and fulfillment to my life.

Emme is an "only child" with six older siblings. This is an interesting dynamic; her next closest sibling is fourteen years older than she is, and none of the six adult children live with us. I refer to our home as a "harmony bubble." We try to put each other first; therefore, everyone's needs are met without anyone having to compete or fight. No, Emme doesn't get to be the sun and moon to us or get what she wants all the time just because she is growing up as an only child. We have learned a lot from raising six children; spoiling them is never a good option.

Darren doesn't ski, and I do. He eats incredibly healthily, so he doesn't love dining out or eating much of my comfort cooking. He has done a lot of self-improvement work but has no interest in going to growth workshops with me. He loves basketball, while I do not. He works out daily; I avoid lifting heavy things and getting sweaty. And while we do many things independently, we both love to travel, take walks, hike, and camp, so there is plenty to do together. Most importantly, we put God first and each other second. We value partnership and do not compete. We understand how blessed we are and, therefore, appreciate each other, flaws and all. We both know the dreams and goals we have for our lives are better and more easily accomplished together than alone.

During my time of self-discovery and personal growth work, I learned everything I could ever want to know about dating, men, and marriage in the work of Allison Armstrong, her company PAX® and her Understanding Men® series. I could write ten more chapters on how my intensive and graduate-level work with her and the PAX Organization has given me the courage and strength to be my best in a truly empowering partnership and marriage. This work has also made me look back on the twenty-five years with Tim and see my part in the ups and downs of our marriage. I can see so many areas where I could have been better. We had a good life together, but there were occasions of conflict and competition instead of building each other up.

I often hear divorced people listing all the character flaws in their exes, and they may very well be correct. But that may lead them to go into new relationships thinking they just need to find the "right" person and never look at their part in the failure of their marriages. Then they bring all that baggage into their next relationship. This simple time spent acknowledging and working on the things each of us can improve in ourselves would probably improve the unfavorable second and third marriage statistics.

My relationship with Darren is not perfect, and I sometimes see behaviors in myself pop up that do not make me proud of myself. It is always a work in progress, and when I see that negative stuff surface, I ask myself what my part was in that argument. When we take this approach, we can take responsibility for what went wrong and work on it moment by moment. One of the best things I have learned through Alison Armstrong's work is that a relationship is defined as a moment of relating. Our relationship is not a separate entity; it is not a thing that can be defined as good or bad, healthy or dysfunctional. It is simply how we relate to each other in every interaction. Choose to relate differently and change the entire relationship. Each interaction can create a downward spiral or can lift us to higher places. This goes for all of our relationships. Do you want to be right and play tit-for-tat, or do you want to take the high road that leads to happiness? You can have an interaction in which you say, "X," which makes him say, "Y," resulting in a battle. Instead, take ownership of trying to improve by changing the way you interact. See if the responses are more favorable over time.

Darren, my husband (which is how his contact is saved in my phone, lol), is an African-American man. So here we are, a biracial couple with a blue-eyed, strawberry-blonde Irish daughter. Sometimes those silly thoughts about what people are thinking come into my consciousness. Darren, in his true, confident, emotional/social/mental/spiritual healthiness, will say, "No one is thinking about you." That comment comes from a sincere and positive frame of mind.

Consider what you see when someone walks past you. You may wonder who they are or notice what they are wearing. The thought lasts about three seconds, and then you go back to what you were doing, where you need to be, what's for dinner, etc. That's how people think about you.

So, our little cohort of three has traveled to the deep south, and we have traveled to South Africa—where our marriage was illegal before 1985. People do a double take on occasion or stare a bit. I could choose to get defensive and hostile, but I have no idea what their thoughts are. So, I just say to myself, *they must think we look good together* and move on without giving it a second more of my attention. After all, they are probably just trying to figure out who our little threesome is.

One time at a rural gas station, I was in the car, and Darren went inside with our granddaughter, her friend, and little Emme, who was about four. As the three African Americans were leaving the store with Emme trailing behind, the clerk, a sweet older lady, came from behind the counter to stop Emme and tell her to wait for her parents. Darren could have become defensive, but he chose to see her as a caring woman who was watching out for a little one. He said, "It's ok, she is with me. Thank you, Ma'am, for being aware and concerned. I appreciate you looking out."

As Emme grows up, people will see her with her dad and know there is a story there that isn't biology. I understand there could be a few challenges. I also know that Darren is preparing her by making sure she knows who she is, that she loves herself, and knows she is loved. She knows he had a choice, and he chose her. The truth is, we rarely get asked about Emme and her African-American father, but we welcome the questions and would be open to that discussion.

I feel good knowing not only will she have someone for daddy/daughter functions but that she will be engaged in future racial diversity conversations as part of the solution. She will be a person who loves and is loved by, respects, and is related to people of two races.

My husband has taught me that we all can choose how we see and interact with others. We can choose to see the worst and be bitter and angry or move on and enjoy the rest of our day. Darren has never needed, nor will he ever need, someone else's protection from anyone trying to make him feel less. No one will ever make him feel that way because he chooses not to allow it.

TOOLS FOR A JOY-FILLED LIFE

Tool # 9

Judgment Is Tricky

Say to yourself daily: *It is none of my business what people think of me.* Then go about your day trying to live by the golden rule, living the life you choose to live.

"Judge not lest ye be judged." (Matthew 7:1 KJV) Have empathy and imagine walking in the shoes of others. Look at yourself in the mirror, stand tall, and remember, unless you are a mind reader, you do not know what people are thinking, so quit making up a story that makes you feel bad.

Andrea Schroll wrote a helpful blog in *Huffpost* called "5 Ways to Overcome Fear of Judgment." I often think of number two in that article when dealing with concerns about what others think. She says, "Resist letting others define you. People will always have an opinion. Understanding that they're entitled to their own thoughts is an important step in moving past any fear of being judged."[17]

In *Judgment Detox*, Gabrielle Bernstein suggests that when you find yourself judging others, simply tell yourself, *I forgive this thought, and I choose again.*[18] I give myself this gentle reminder regularly. We all do it; we make snap insinuations about someone we see. We must notice, accept, and be aware of this to change that behavior in ourselves and stop it in the future. The idea here is that the first step is to stop judging yourself. Next, understand it is human to care about what others think; it is impossible to stop caring altogether. Plus, disregarding what people think creates a lack of self-awareness and stunts growth. The final step is to only be concerned with the opinions of those people whom you love and respect, who live their lives as you seek to live. You are putting yourself out in the world, inviting criticism, and working to make your dreams come true. You must only concern yourself with the opinions of others doing the same.

EIGHT
PUZZLE PIECES

Life is like a puzzle. Only if you fit the pieces to the right places, you will see the beauty of it.

—Dave Nahar

With everything I have experienced, I sometimes feel as if there should be no more tough stuff for me. Then another painful thing happens. In fact, the reason I have time to write is that I'm facing another difficult period. That is the truth of the human experience—the longer we live, the more tough stuff we will face. As I have said before, this tough stuff is the invitation for growth through what tough teaches us.

This challenge is more than I could have prepared for. I have worked through plenty of entrepreneurial struggles through the years. Through each, I questioned whether I could survive the downslide of the roller coaster, but in most, I had some control. At this particular time, the only thing I feel I can control is my mindset.

Life changed for everyone when the world shut down in March 2020. The hospitality and live event industries were hit particularly hard. Fun Productions' typical events include corporate picnics, conventions, conferences, high school, college, and social events. Each event hosts one hundred to two thousand guests. We went from having our best year to date in 2019 to being completely shut down, with our entire team furloughed in 2020.

I continued to pay general and administrative expenses with our cash reserves, but with zero revenue coming in, we had to keep expenses to a minimum. I missed my team and their energy. I tried to remember that some small business owners had lost everything or lost loved ones. To them, my broken business would be a dream, but sitting in that feeling of brokenness was still hard.

I felt like this might finally be the flood that took me down, the proverbial back-breaking straw. This time of uncertainty and fear of losing the business took me to rock bottom. I knew life would never be the same. I was angry, and I felt defeated. Through no fault of my own, my business was on the verge of bankruptcy after 30 years of grinding hardcore to keep it successfully growing. I would hear people say things like, "Oh, small businesses got all that government bailout. They are fine." That was like a knife in my heart. The truth is the government assistance would have lasted me about 30 days with no revenue coming in. I had to sell my building, sell trucks, have an auction of equipment, and not pay a single employee during the pandemic just to cover basic expenses for the 15 months of 98% of revenue being gone.

The uncertainty and lack of control invited me to make a choice. I could sit here and drown in my misery or find higher ground. It occurred to me that we typically think of rock bottom as near the end of our rope, like near-death—super-extreme moments. They do not always have to be the extreme kind, but maybe they are.

I am grateful that, to date, I have not been near death, homeless, strung out, or in prison. However, I have been at rock bottom a few times in my years on this planet. As I define rock bottom, it is a breaking point that becomes trans-formative; a time when you cannot keep going on like this, and you have been given this moment as a wake-up call that says, *seriously, girl! What better sign do you need to stop the BS and do something about this?* I look at these moments as invitations—granted, not the pretty, embossed, celebratory, come-join-us type of invitation, but still an invitation. The invitation hits you square in the head and knocks you over, comes with some sobbing, and it says, *hey, it is time to make a change, or you are going to lose your shit, sister.*

When you think of it this way, you can get out from under the cloud and see it as a bright, sunshiny awakening that spurs new thoughts: *Thank God you can stop this sub-par existence. It is no longer just drizzling; the floodgates are open, the water is rising, and you are drowning. So now, instead of walking around wet all the time, trying to step between raindrops, you have no choice but to grab a bucket or move to higher ground.*

I had been running a business that was no longer fulfill-ing me simply because it was never painful enough to stop doing it. It has provided a life that has been awesome and full of experiences, relationships, and opportunities, but it is no longer ideal for me personally. Using the rain analogy, it was as if 50% of the time, it was dry and only partly cloudy, and now and then, it was bright blue skies; but occasionally, it was a torrential downpour of not fitting for me. Then the sun would come out just enough for me to keep going again. In fact, there were many times of bliss and enjoyment. Then there were moments of utter despair that forced me to make enough small changes to improve it so that it worked fine again. Here I was, in the third quarter of 2020, running an event business with no events and no team because of

Covid-19. The signs were obvious enough that I could never go back to life the way it was again.

This realization caused me to finally stop floundering and hand over restarting the business to my son, Josh. It turned out to be easy for me to relinquish control because the business was basically already gone. It was Josh's turn to see if he could make it. I was forced to stop dabbling in what I wanted to do for my career and start taking some new risks without the safety net of Fun Productions. As I started to emerge from the anger and fear, I could see how this giant setback would be another blessing. Josh, as a second-generation owner, will get to deal with the hard work of starting a business. He will have to wear all the hats because he does not have a team to do payroll, pay the bills, run events, and do sales. Additionally, he will wear the badge of honor for rebuilding.

As I complete this book, the business faucet has been turned on again. Josh has been incredibly fortunate to see several team members come back. Their return is a testament to hiring people aligned with our values and who felt successful at their jobs because of the EOS process. After working other jobs for almost two years, these people chose to return. Josh has learned most of what he needs to know. He understands his passion and his strengths and has the wisdom to hand off the other tasks to those who are uniquely able to do them. And he will make his own mistakes and have his lessons in being an entrepreneur.

EOS helped us survive the shutdown. Even when it was only Josh and me, we had Level 10 Meetings™ and used the time to accomplish bite-sized goals. These projects made us much stronger, and we may never have had the time to accomplish that without the pandemic. We have new and improved systems, software, and processes for the new normal. We had to make hard decisions to stay afloat.

It is interesting to look at one's life—the highs and lows—and watch the puzzle come together. I am blessed to have learned that I am the sum of my experiences, both good and bad. I find I rely on the grit of being raised in instability. Because of my life quake, my passion is helping leaders understand that their business is not their life, just a piece of it. I love helping them create a business that runs efficiently without them sacrificing their lives for it. I love working with married partners and family businesses to help them learn how they can have conflict in a productive and healthy way. My experiences allow me the honor of helping business owners and their teams rise out of chaos to make their work the catalyst for the life they want. Every what, why, and who of my life are the puzzle pieces that brought me to a place of purpose and passion to do what I was put here to do. I want the same for you!

I think small businesses can make a social impact and positive change, and I want to help owners understand their impact. My goal for small business teams is to have *The EOS Life*—doing what they love, with people they love; making a huge impact; being compensated appropriately; and having time for other passions so they can look back on a life well lived.

One of the most important things I have learned in over a century on this planet is that it is in times of strife and struggle that we can come out the other side better than we were before. I believe God uses these hard times when we feel broken to transform us into a much better version of ourselves. When we are in broken pieces, we often pray to be like we were before, and that is selling God short. I believe He wants to improve us, not just fix us. I am fortunate enough to have a Pastor in my life that showed me this concept through the analogy of Kintsugi. This is the Japanese art of fixing broken glass objects by adding gold to the glue. The word Kintsugi is translated as "to join with gold." What becomes of a broken glass bowl when the pieces are put back together with gold is now a unique piece of art, no longer just a simple bowl. The spiritual meaning is about forgiveness and self-love. It is about accepting ourselves with our cracks and flaws and seeing how much more beautiful we become with the scars.

I was recently preparing to be a guest on a podcast. I think the list of questions I was given and my answers will be a good conclusion.

- **If you could tell your teenage self anything, what would you say?**

  Find out who you are and be that! Be grateful for your blessings. See every struggle as a place that will help you grow and look for the lessons instead of complaining about how difficult it is. And most importantly, stop judging yourself and talking badly to yourself. Treat yourself with the grace and kindness you reserve for your dearest friends.

- **What do you wish you would have known before starting your career?**

  Checking boxes and accomplishing things do not give you more value. You were born with extreme value and everything you need to live out your purpose. You do not have to prove you are worthy. You were born; therefore, you are worthy. At the end of your days, you won't find yourself wishing that you could get a few more things done. You might, however, wish you spent more time with the people you love.

- **How do you stay motivated when things are not going the way you need them to or how you had hoped?**

  I remember my "*why*": my core focus, purpose, cause, and passion. I do not get up every morning to score goals and deposit checks. I get up every morning to live out my purpose, and if I am doing that every day, then I am successful. If I am doing my best to love and have faith, then I am already successful in being purposeful, and the rest just comes. That is motivating for me.

FINAL THOUGHTS

My entire life story seems to be lesson after lesson to teach me that I am not in control. That life is meant to be a ride, but not a ride on easy street. Life is supposed to be hard sometimes. It is our job to lean into the hard and feel the pain, not numb it, deny it, or be a victim of it. It is our job to take the good and appreciate it while also taking the hard—with the same level of gratitude—and learn from it. My hope for all of you is that you take life by the horns and live it all out. That you run towards the things that scare you. That you figure out who you are and be that. That you discover your passions and live them boldly. Do not ever hide from fully living due to fear of what might be hard. The hard parts will be your biggest chance to grow and become your best.

As I wrote this book, I struggled with being authentic and vulnerable and balancing my truth with the need to protect other people in my life. Not every truth made it to these pages. I didn't omit them because I am ashamed or trying to hide those truths. I chose to leave a few things out for one of the following two reasons.

1. I can only tell my story. Although their stories touched mine, and those people I love have profoundly affected me and taught me many things, their stories are not my stories to tell. The privacy of people not

choosing to write a book about their lives deserves to be maintained.

2. The story is still happening. As of this writing, I am in the middle of more life, more difficult things, more joy, and more life lessons. Because I am still sometimes in the middle of something challenging, I am not sure of what the light on the other side will look like yet and what it will have to teach me. I cannot write about a story that is not finished yet.

I leave you with a summarized list of the Tools for a Joy-Filled Life—my most critical mantras:

1. Let go of limiting beliefs holding you back.
2. Take responsibility for your decisions, your actions, and your life.
3. Manage your expectations of yourself and others.
4. Don't let anyone dash your dreams or define you. Be intentional with who you share this life with.
5. Have a plan and remember there is help; don't try to do it all alone.
6. You can't control everything.
7. Be grateful, and deal with the feelings while learning from it all.
8. Find out who you are, then do that well!
9. Do not fear judgment, try not to judge, and belong where your authentic self belongs, so you do not spend your life trying to fit in.

ACKNOWLEDGMENTS

I acknowledge that the "Tools for Joy" in this book are not my original thoughts. Most of what I have learned, put into practice, or shared in this book I did not create alone. But the experiences, mistakes made, and stories are mine to share. I thank many brilliant minds for putting their thoughts, research, and help into the world so that people like me can learn to live better lives.

Darren, my husband: thank you for being my safe place where I seek wisdom and find perspective when things become tough. Thank you for loving me as I am and being my partner on this ride. I can do what I do and be what I am because you are who you are. I love you.

To my beautiful, God-created children: I am honored and privileged to be your mom. Joshua, Hogan, and Emmerson, you are each unique, and I love each of you the same amount in different ways. Your individual, distinct, and amazing strengths are gifts to me. You continue to teach me how to rise to new challenges and be a better person. My underlying goal is to raise my ceiling because it is your floor. Keep being you—you do that better than anyone else.

The Women Presidents Organization has been my community. Thank you to the Denver Chapter Sisters. Your beauty, grace, wisdom, intelligence, vulnerability, achievements, and friendship have lifted me many times. You inspire me with your accomplishments and how you continue to excel and thrive through hardship. Thank you, Pam, Sharon, Mona, Jennifer, Wendy, Lorena, Erica, Monique, Heather, Marla, Lisa, Karen, Blakelee, Tamra, and Gretchen, and a special thanks to Brenda, my mentor, coach, and our group's fearless leader.

I've been fortunate to have been part of the hospitality and special-event industry community for many years. Thank you all for your pizzazz, creativity, glam, attention to detail, and passion. It has been a joy to be part of an industry so full of life. The world needs you because humans must gather and celebrate. You will always have an important place in the world. A special shout out to Syd Sexton, who has been my sounding board and genuine friend. Thank you for pushing me years ago to write. I appreciate you showing up for me when things are hard. Another special thank you goes to Ingrid Nagy, my friend, hotel roomie, and International Live Event Association (ILEA) mentor. I have always looked up to you and am better for trying to emulate you. More thanks go to the CEO group: Cal, Pat, Cindy, Alex, Ann, Pam, Bonnie, and Tracey. Your advice, wisdom, and sharing through the years have been priceless.

Years with the great staff at Fun Productions have garnered all my appreciation and respect. Thank you to all who dedicated your time, talents, and amazing work to grow a place where I am proud to have been a part.

To the EOS Implementer Community™, you have my utmost gratitude for being brilliant and abundance-minded individuals who Live the EOS Core Values of doing what you say, helping first, being humbly confident, growing so you don't die, and doing the right thing. I am honored to be part of a tribe of people who continue to inspire me, make me proud of what I do, and help me live The EOS Life.

Now, for all the thought leaders, authors, and exceptional minds who have given me the tools and knowledge to continue to strive to become my best self, I hold you in great esteem. You continue to make a dramatic difference in the lives of those who seek your knowledge:

The collective writers of the only book of original thought. Merely opening the Bible gives me peace, and y'all, every life lesson and piece of advice you need is on those pages. It is the original self-help manual, teaching us how to live, love, and be better.

Gino Wickman, you are a true visionary who has changed the lives of millions of business owners and leaders by sharing the tools to simplify, increase abundance, clarify vision, and calm chaos.

Patrick Lencioni, your business and fable-writing genius have helped shape teams, leaders, and organizations through your thought leadership. I am thankful to have read your brilliance during my entrepreneurial journey.

Dr. Brené Brown, thank you for caring so deeply for all things human and for sharing your life's work with us. You have illuminated and given us the language and tools to address all those things we have kept in the dark. Through your help in giving us all "the courage to show up," we are better humans, families, leaders, and communities.

Simon Sinek, I am in awe of your brain. Thank you for showing us that until we get in touch with our "why," we can never live up to our higher calling and purpose.

Alison Armstrong, thank you for your lifetime of dedication to your work in *Making Sense of Men© and Understanding Women©*. Without your continued curiosity and desire to help humanity, I and so many others would not have found love and partnership. You taught us how to seek understanding and partners outside the biology of our human animal to get to the beauty of our Human Spirit.

APPENDIX/ADDITIONAL RESOURCES

Please use this QR code to go to an online Resource site

Please use this QR Code for your free Map of Me Download

Please use this QR Code for your free E-Book: My Business Blunders

ENDNOTES

1. Anne Lamott, *Bird by Bird* (Knopf Doubleday Publishing Group; 1st Paperback Edition September 1, 1995) also referenced by Brené Brown, *Rising Strong* (New York, NY: Random House, 2017).
2. Jim Dethmer, Diana Chapman, Kaley Warner Klemp, *The 15 Commitments of Conscious Leadership* (Dethmer, Chapman, and Klemp, 2015).
3. PsychCentral Online Article *How to Relinquish Unrealistic Expectations: 4 Tips,* Medically reviewed by Matthew Boland, PhD — By Margarita Tartakovsky, MS — Updated on Jun 16, 2022
4. Healthline Article *You're Not a Fraud. Here's How to Recognize and Overcome Imposter Syndrome.* Medically reviewed by Vara Saripalli, Psy.D. — By Crystal Raypole on April 16, 2021
5. Darren Hardy, *The Compound Effect* (New York, NY: Vanguard Press, 2010).
6. Van Doorn Ph.D., Maarten. "You Are the Average of the Five People You Spend the Most Time with." *Maarten van Doorn, Ph.D.* June 20, 2018. https://maartenvandoorn.medium.com/you-are-the-average-of-the-five-people-you-spend-the-most-time-with-a2ea32d08c72
7. Winter, Catherine. "How to Let Go of Control: 8 No-Nonsense Tips!" *A Conscious Rethink.* Last modified June 9, 2022. www.aconsciousrethink.com/7151/let-go-of-control/.
8. Horton, Anisa Purbasari. "Five Mindfulness Techniques for Letting Go of Control." *Fast Company.* November 11, 2019.

9. Bruce Feiler. *Life is in the Transitions* (New York, NY: Penguin Press, 2020).

10. Brown, Brené. "Brené Brown on Joy and Gratitude." *The Global Leadership Network*. November 21, 2018. www.globalleadership. org/articles/leading-yourself/brene-brown-on-joy-and-gratitude/.

11. "Giving Thanks Can Make You Happier." *Harvard Health Publishing*. August 14, 2021. https://www.health.harvard.edu/ healthbeat/giving-thanks-can-make-you-happier.

12. "10 Amazing Statistics to Celebrate National Gratitude Month." *Halo*. October 19, 2020. www.halo.com/10-amazing-statistics-to-celebrate-national-gratitude-month/.

13. Chernoff, Marc. "10 Ways Happy People Choose Happiness." *Marc and Angel Tool Life*. March 1, 2012. www.marcandangel. com/2012/03/01/10-ways-happy-people-choose-happiness.

14. Susan David, Ph.D., Emotional Agility: Get Unstuck, Embrace Change, and Thrive in Work and Life (New York, NY: Penguin Publishing Group, 2016).

15. Lois Mowday Rabey, *When Your Soul Aches: Hope and Help for Women Who Have Lost Their Husbands* (Colorado Springs, CO: Waterbrook, 2000).

16. Johnson Cornell College of Business https://www.johnson.cornell.edu/smith-family-business-initiative-at-cornell/resources/family-business-facts/#:~: text=Business%20Survey%202012).-,The%20average%20 life%20span%20of%20a%20family%2Downed%20 business%20is,Businessweek.com%2C%202010)

17. Schroll, Andrea. "5 Ways to Overcome Fear of Judgement." *HuffPost*. Last Modified June 14, 2017. https://www.huffpost.com/ entry/5-ways-to-overcome-fear-of-judgment_b_10396254.

18. Gabrielle Bernstein, *Judgment Detox* (New York, NY: Gallery Books, 2018).

ABOUT THE AUTHOR

 Dawn Abbott grew her start-up from nothing to a multi-office, 14,000-square-foot warehouse, and showroom. Her focus was on being a good leader who engages and empowers her team toward success. After tragedy struck in 2013, Dawn was faced with some serious decisions to make. Her grieving period caused a reflection that created a major mindset shift.

This process brought her to becoming an EOS Implementer, where Dawn has found her true gifts, strengths, and purpose in Speaking, Coaching, Facilitation, and Training. She knows the process for helping leaders get what they want from their businesses and their lives. Dawn is passionate about giving small business owners the permission to live a life that includes their family & friends, their passions, the time freedom, and the money that they want and need.

Dawn currently resides in Colorado with her husband and their daughter. The couple also has a blended family of 6 adult children and 5 businesses between them.

GET THE TOOLS YOU'VE BEEN LOOKING FOR TO EMPOWER AND GROW YOUR BUSINESS

BOOK A DISCOVERY CALL!

Abbott Coaching

I invite you on a journey of self-discovery and personal growth, into ever-increasing authenticity and self-love.

I created my personal Map of Me to help guide my decisions from a place of strength. My Map of Me has awakened me to who I really am, and who I want to be. It allows me to live from my design at my highest and best, as well as plan to shore up the weaknesses—and it's given me the ability to see and appreciate the differences. I believe that all individuals should be authentic, open and able to express themselves fully with confidence—your Map of Me is your guide for doing just that.

MAP OF ME

10 STEPS TO LIVING INTENTIONALLY

Abbott
Coaching

SCAN CODE TO DOWNLOAD

JOIN OUR EXCLUSIVE BUSINESS GROWTH COMMUNITY TODAY!

Don't miss out on the opportunity to be part of our thriving community of ambitious professionals. By opting in to our database, you'll gain access to exclusive professional & personal coaching content designed to help you achieve your goals and maximize your potential.

SCAN CODE TO SUBSCRIBE

**FOLLOW DAWN ON SOCIAL MEDIA
AND GAIN CLARITY AND ALIGNMENT**

ABBOTTCOACH.COM

Printed in the USA
CPSIA information can be obtained
at www.ICGtesting.com
LVHW011003090124
768323LV00077B/1582/J

'